# OUT OF LAND

# OUT OF LAND

New & Selected Poems

## LAWRENCE SAIL

BLOODAXE BOOKS

ISBN: 1 85224 183 7

First published 1992 by
Bloodaxe Books Ltd,
P.O. Box 1SN,
Newcastle upon Tyne NE99 1SN.


Bloodaxe Books Ltd acknowledges
the financial assistance of Northern Arts.

Cover printing by J. Thomson Colour Printers Ltd, Glasgow.

Printed in Great Britain by
Cromwell Press Ltd, Broughton Gifford, Melksham, Wiltshire.

*for Matthew and Erica*

# Acknowledgements

This book includes poems selected from Lawrence Sail's previous collections: *Opposite Views* (Dent, 1974), *The Drowned River* (Mandeville Press, 1978), *The Kingdom of Atlas* (Secker & Warburg, 1980), *Devotions* (Secker & Warburg, 1987) and *Aquamarine* (Gruffyground Press, 1988).

Acknowledgements are due to the editors of the following publications in which some of the new poems in the fourth section of this book were first published: *Encounter, London Magazine, The Observer, Otter, Owl, Oxford Magazine, The Poetry Book Society Anthology 1988-89* (PBS/Hutchinson, 1988), *Poetry Book Society Anthology: 1* (PBS/Hutchinson, 1990), *Poetry Durham, PN Review, Poetry Review, Poetry Voice, The Spectator, Stand, Stonechat* (Stride Press, 1992). 'Rose Garden' was first published in *First and Always* (Faber, 1988). 'Recurrent' was broadcast on *Poetry Now* (BBC Radio 3). 'Elements' was printed by John Randle of the Whittington Press as four posters in a series of sixteen published by the Friends of the Cheltenham Festival of Literature (1989, 1990, 1991, 1992).

# Contents

## NEW POEMS

FROM **OPPOSITE VIEWS**
(1974)

## Expatriate Teacher

I bring you the symbols of alien gods
From northern kingdoms weathered by the wind,
Where history lingers, though long ago destroyed
By word and war, by shapely post-war words.

I tell you of illuminated scripts,
The Roman Forum, the statues at Versailles:
Our tendency to build elaborate forms
Beyond our substance, outliving time and pain.

You walk to school barefoot, on stony paths;
By wind-sharp thorn you see the jackal move,
Biding its time. At night the cattle shift
Uneasily beneath the sullen moon.

What use are books and marble, when the senses
Go numb and fail to warn of coming danger?
At home you shed your blazer, casting off
The Latin motto they stitched across your heart.

# Migrants

Midnight. Wheels still squeal in the lane.
Further up the coast, the lay-bys
Will be blockaded with caravans, cars,
Dinghies, dormobiles, trucks and trailers:
Estates of nomads improvising sleep,
Their minds awash in tides of passing lights.

For others keep on, unwilling to lose –
Except for petrol, tea, a smoke,
A pee, a gulp of fatty air –
A moment. They postpone their dreams
Till, parked in rows along the front, they let
The dimly shifting ocean lull them loose.

Behind them dust resettles, calm
Laps through their curtained houses, clearing
A year's flotsam. Journeying on
They head for home: new letters dealt
Untidily across the hall and, beyond,
The kindly futures of those sea-swept rooms.

# Death of a Child

It lay beyond the tidy garden ways –
An endless world where wicked berries gleamed
Precisely in the seasonless disorder;
With leaves like flags hoisted to dizzy treetops,
Cables of creeper a foot thick. A place
Where nothing was settled, nothing tamely focussed
To prim gravel, a few labelled roses.
He noticed that this area shared with others
The name of 'no', selected by his parents.

The parents, who often later blamed themselves,
Smiled as he tested boundaries through four summers.
The potting shed was good while it lasted, the trees
Easily bore his weight – and when those palled,
It was time to help him make his own small garden:
A replica of father's, ten feet square,
With regular rows and space to walk between.
He liked it when they knelt to dig his garden,
Seeing behind their heads the great space no.

In the fifth year, beneath the splaying orchids,
The opposite view had equal fascination –
Looking back, he could barely define the zone
Of barren ground in which his parents stooped,
Peering, calling, anxious to know where he was.
But he was no, all made of shiny tubers,
With berry eyes and skin smooth as leaves,
Twigs for fingers and a dark mind. In delight
He shouted his name, fled down the unfenced ways.

And when, breathless, he paused, it seemed to him
He stood at his own true threshold – a cool clearing
Of grass and lily flowers, at whose still centre
Bamboo had formed a graceful canopy.
The light still held, he had only to cross.
From the first step forward, he felt the ground give way
In recognition: boldly, with joy, he trod
Into the reed-covered lake. They found him there,
His eyes still bright, staring beyond their world.

# A Grandmother's Album

And here they are again, collecting shells.
They often do things like that. Look at their heads:
Good heads, I think. They are bending over the pool.
They love their father. In winter he also goes with them,
Makes animals by packing the frozen snow.

Here, in fact, is a rabbit. Isn't it good?
And now, a bear – the polar kind, of course –
It really looks as if it will fall and smother
All the family. He's clever with his hands,
My son. I think he's doing very well.

Each year he sends me pictures such as these.
I keep them for the longer winter evenings.
Sometimes, at night, I see my grandchildren's faces
Right above me – their pale blue eyes which peer
Calmly into the stillness where I live.

# Adjustment

Another one dying, not five yards away –
A wrinkled suit, slowly deflating
As blood disperses through level streets;
Shoes vertical, massive as skis,
Stubbing their toes against cut stone.

Each focussed detail should scream in the mind,
Hairs which the razor missed that morning,
Breast-pocket biro, ring on stiff finger:
Perhaps there are letters in one of the pockets,
A picture even? Relax, it's a body.

Besides, the experts will soon arrive
To comfort the broken-hearted, explain
The basic trends and historical reasons –
Wise and gentle men, intoning
The litany of the accepted fact.

Helpless we watch, bewitched by the constant
Seepage of life – so numb with sensation
That it's only our dad who leaps up in alarm
To adjust the sensitive tuner, growling
'That's never the colour of real blood.'


## Fisherman


Out past the twinkling land there rides a craft
Hove to and steeply rocking in the sea.
One barely glimpsed, at paying out the nets
Which all his life have been his life, reflects
How many nights like this one have washed aft
As tides flood in and ebb, as silently.

But as he reaches to clear the tarry strands
He sees the water, black beyond his hands
And pauses. Rough hands grasping at his own
Pull steadily, not inwards now but down.

# One of the Unfit

You lie lassoed, within the mountain's shadow,
By the grey tide which smothered you from behind –
And you didn't even turn.

Nothing but a periscope horn, driving forward
To plough the sulphur and siphon down old codes
For your silted brain – the tang of the desert rose,
The long dust of the herd heading for water,
Suns and moons drifting above your head.
This and a ripple of ribs just breaking surface
Deft scavengers have polished, ashes preserved.

The brain was always limited, confined
Short of the plain's horizon, warped by heat,
Even immediate vision blurred with flies.
Danger could only assume a known form,
Low as a lion, or between the hyena's sprung jaws.
But this? The earth gave food, was nothing more
Than sweet, white grass, memento and promise of rain.

I see you fatally lamed by disbelief,
Scarcely feeling the scalding flow round your ankles
As the grey tide overtook you.

# Legacy

The pictures are left and, most of all, that subject
You painted so often, of broad-ribbed boats on a shore.
No pleasure-boats, these, to bob by planks on wheels,
But massive, made from the memories of storms,
Deeply rooted far in the sand's dry depths.

Not once did you face them seaward, paint in canvas,
Or bring the flickering foam to lift their bows.

And then that island – in early versions it lay
Like a misplaced cloud across the even water;
So light it would surely lift and drift with the first
Fine wind. Later, it swelled to a chalky scarp,
Became treacherous, acquired a hostile summit.

There were never people or houses on your island:
Blank as an iceberg, it cut clean through horizons.

In time, the boats climbed higher up the beach;
No tide could touch them, not even one freak breaker
Reclaim their hulking walls. And all this while
The island grew, diminishing sea and sky,
Yet always drifting further out of reach.

I often think how through thirty years of marriage,
War and remarriage, you illustrated defeat.

# Apart

'I have made the chicken last through a fourth day.
There is no panic. The washing will soon get done.
The draining-board is clear. Nothing has happened.'
Each evening when you ring, I make the effort
To sound unruffled – just as you also sound
From a hundred miles away; your voice so gentle
It seems you are afraid to bruise my eardrum.

When our words drift over counties, nothing is hard –
Affections jam the exchange, extravagant silence
Becomes a gift to distribute in between words.
We span the dangerous distance with tokens of love:
In case the car should crash, the aeroplane fly
Too near the sun, the survivor have to face
The end of pride, beginnings of a conscience.

With mouth and ear alone we bring about
A miracle of intimate relations.
Invisibly we blossom, you becoming
The perfect wife I always knew you were,
While I send forests of flowers to where you're staying
And think how lucky I am, recalling my mother
Boiling an egg for her supper, again and again.

The day we do not speak, the house will look
Suddenly grubby, everything out of place,
Chicken-bones everywhere. Oversleeping, I'll wake
To hear the doorbell wrenched from its socket and just
Have time to dash downstairs, fumble the lock.
After that, the disappointment lasts
Only till both have forgotten and then remembered.

# Guidelines

good afternoon and welcome come this way
here on the ground floor im sorry no dogs or prams
to your left the two imposing busts portray
the marquis and his wife they were executed
by bartolini yes they look content maam
as well they might do having instituted
eleven sons each with his monogram

the library contains twelve thousand tomes
mostly unread and thus in fine condition
while the famous tapestry hanging opposite comes
from bruges and shows us cupid as he cheers
two noble lovers on to coy coition
the fireplace of course is adam the chandelier
french one of the ninth earls acquisitions

the sofa here in the drawingroom was a gift
from catherine the great to the fourteenth count
dont miss the stuccoed ceiling here is the lift
installed by the national trust and made in preston
in nineteen thirty five here we dismount
to view the bedrooms continue our ingestion
of useless facts in staggering amounts

this fine fourposter the last heir occupied
a bishop who had it carved with every spire
within the diocese and later died
in italy from a painful stomach gout
to be precise in some poor peasants byre
who wouldnt house a heretic being devout
a turn of the wheel one cannot but admire

the rest you can see for yourselves the original lock
on the sixteenth century chest the silverware
sevres vases mirrors screens and clocks
untouched by hand roped off in holy precincts
dynastic gods preserved in musty air
note the virginal with its quite distinct
keyboard of nails and strings of human hair

our tour ends here for those of you who plan
a second visit dont forget a supply
of matches petrol even grenades if you can
youll find me waiting away from the house and drive
behind damp walls where my family serves and dies
after two hundred years still stubborn enough to survive
kept warm by a dream of flames climbing roofhigh


# Landfall


No course of ours had steered to that inland state,
No special grace, or confluence of currents
Engineering new levels. Yet both of us –
You, with hair unwound on the moonwhite pillow,
Calmly taking my gaze; and I at last
Free of questions – knew we had never before,
Being seafarers, journeyed so far from water.

Later, I tried to piece the route together,
Searching in vain for clues – the day had passed
Much as another. Minor panics, doorbells,
A baby cutting teeth, a finger cut
And bandaged, nothing more. The usual rise
And usual fall of circumstance, which leave
Slowly evolving ruins along the shore.

It still disturbs me that there should be no chart
Or tidy compass bearing by which to locate
That island of ourselves above the litter
Marooned by daily tides. But slowly I'm learning
How love, like moonlight, may not be achieved –
Only, as in the ocean's timeless turning,
Be followed through its own slow rhythms and received.

# The Return

This is the house to which you came back
After your mother died,
These the roseheads pitted with black,
Once her pride.

Here is the door through which you passed
Into the echoing hall
Where gleaming mercury trapped in glass
Predicted rainfall.

Up these stairs which she dusted and swept
Daily, you climbed to bed:
Beside your unwashed pillow, you kept
The book she read.

And this cracked mirror is one in which
Her image beckoned to you
The night they found you drowned in a ditch,
Gazing through.

# A Picture by Klee

X-rayed against the double night
Of the cut moon and the dwarf sun,
The wire frames of your skeleton town
Might have been gutted by fire, or nudged
Askew by earthquake.

But over the leaning towers, bright flags
Semaphore their messages
Of occupation, refuse to submit
To natural disaster, or
Random history.

No town was ever so ruined, or sited
So far beyond the reach of weather,
The limits of naming: yet each step taken
Along its deserted streets, provokes
Familiar echoes.

For this is the fossil Troy embedded
In all our minds: the child's first sketch
Of heaven, the old man's Holy City,
Clear as glass. The first and last
Possible settlement.

# Alternatives

In this house, today, I must face again
The consequences of that first betrayal:
The quick division of cells,
The envious opposite numbers
Which, since our birth, have counted out whole deserts
Between the brief oases of satisfaction.

Either, to stay behind these familiar doors,
Gathering data, wreaking no further damage,
And teach myself in time
How to grow into the walls:
One day, then, calmly to be absorbed
Into the fabric of my well-stocked tomb.

Or, bravely imperfect, to disperse along
This way or that, carpet-bag stuffed with patents,
In search of anonymous lakes,
Peaks undivided by names:
To become a mapper of mirages, an intimate
Of roadside verges, expert at meeting strangers.

Either, my heirs at last allowed to cross
Into the stuffy room where they lost a father:
Or further expeditions,
Pursued through generations,
Pushing a few yards on from that last failure
Of dilettante parents crazed by sun.

Either, or – in my father's house I weigh
The mutually balanced forces of deduction.
And this is the worst fear:
To think how sons and fathers
Might cancel each other out, their warring minds
Fall to zero, for want of either madness.

## After the Reunion

The following day, I saw you once more –
Making your way through thin rain
Past grey college walls, back to the train;
Suitcase in hand, your face gripped
By worry, as if something had slipped
Your mind, which memory could not restore.

Stopped by the lights, I watched you cross
A few feet ahead – forgetting that,
Even through glass, a stare attracts
Attention. You looked up, surprised,
And quickly down again, your eyes
Unwilling to focus nine years' loss.

'Christ!' You had said at the dinner, 'It's great
To meet again!' – and out they came,
The stale old jokes, forgotten names,
River parties, escapades:
Your past, like college silver, displayed
Intact inside its walled estate.

You really did expect to trace
Those common threads, across the maze
Of marriage, children, jobs, decay –
And vainly I tried, as others did,
To fool you, nodded agreement and hid
Embarrassment under a smiling face.

Now, disappointed, you gave me this last
Reproving look. Then amber, green:
Tyremarks where your tracks had been.
Driving on, I wondered who
Had best played Judas, me or you:
You to the present, or I to the past.

# Approaches to the Sea

The clifftop walker, taking the air,
Admires the sea: a distant view
Of blank blue miles, where scallops of sunlight
Skim the eye, and perhaps a boat
Tastefully bobs from bay to bay.
But watching, under the folding swell,
The slow, immensely patient body
Flex its muscles, he feels his head
Grow giddy with wheeling gulls.

Half a day out, the passenger leans
Over the rails, as the liner throbs
Its scheduled way across fair weather,
Stitching a herring-bone hem on glass.
Master of deck-games and nautical terms,
Serenely he rides – till the clouting waves
Abolish dances and close down the bar.
Hunched in his bunk then, he hears the veneer
Crack in the pitching staterooms.

The floating bather, flatly pinned
Against the sea, squints at the sky,
Enjoying a calm sensation of poise.
He cannot gauge, on the thin border
Of air and water, what leeway he makes,
Or feel the fingering currents pass
His body along. Already his feet
Are softly dissolving. Enclosing tides
Make straight for his splayed bones.

Goggle-eyed, the diver flashes
Down through sunlight into darkness –
Quick as a fish with his rubber feet,
His streamlined body piercing the flows.
Feelers reach from the weedbed, to time
His bottled pulse, fish-eyes follow
His acrobatics, unimpressed,
Seeing strapped to his black back
The limits of his affinity.

Cartwheeling down the endless fathoms,
Unwrapping through his slow descent,
The drowning man escapes comparisons.
Clifftop walker, passenger, bather,
Diver – he sees them all as they were,
Alien phantoms long marooned
Out of their element. Gladly he feels
His lungs flood with knowledge, his mind
Sprout prehistoric gills.


## Revival


Nothing escapes me: lying here under the wrappings,
With feet and hands raised to a peak, I share
Each twitch of twilight, can sense the surrounding air
Set gelatine thick with the sweetness of wallflowers, trapping
Drifts of seeds in its finely meshed snare.

Each precious detail homes to my cool tent –
The ringdove gloating in the wood, the tethered rose
Folding itself into sleep; moonlight which glows
Blue in blowball mantles; a dry adjustment
Of wingbones in the snagged and winding hedgerow.

Butterflies wink on my eyelids, wings revive
My sluggish heart. Slowly, whole landscapes infect
Each stretch of tissue. Already I can detect
The lapdog shifting beneath my heels – the live
Tickle of beard across my marble gullet.

FROM **THE KINGDOM OF ATLAS**
(1980)

# Alphabet Soup

The sunken letters keep their options,
scarcely evolved in a soapy broth
where the last word on any subject
melts to an anagram of moonshine,
literal truth.

No given usage quite wears them out:
consumed, they might be the sacrament
of pride swallowed – or, stirred, resettle
oh in omens, telling the future
in new last words.

Innocent as messengers they stand
by, are only bearers of the word –
already looking elsewhere, as we
try to break the rosy seals, to get
at real meaning.

## At Tone Vale

Here beyond dark shrubs
past the board warning
HANDICAPPED CHILDREN
love becomes touch, where
theology fails,
where the word was never
a beginning.

And it comes at you
fiercely, love jerking
with quick monkey-hands
from its confinements,
plucking, demanding
more than an even heart,
a blurted tear.

Brittle as the steel
which props them, they are
true monsters of love,
these children who still
are waving madly
as we hobble away
in search of words.

# The Poet Reclining, 1915

His eyes like dark fruit-stones
turn away, in sleep
or slow seep of power –
not loss, but transference.

Stretched at the meadow's margin
in washes of lush grass,
with hands folded he praises
the faithful hinterland;
its logs in low stockades,
pagodas of dark evergreens,
every gift of stillness
that enables the safe grazing
of a sheep and a large horse.

Only, over a shed,
topping the trees of Russia,
a sky of lilac bruisemarks
heads for the Winter Palace.

## Children in Snow

White fritterings,
the hedges pasted high
with glue: and the land drifting
up to a darkness which flares
like blue gas at the rim.

Our children step
easily into it:
too small for comparisons
they ride absolutes simply,
printing with their red boots.

In the distance
we see them jerk and slip,
fooled by the least tip of slope:
delighted dwarves, they welcome
each new loss of balance.

Beaded curtains
fall between them and us.
They will come back, we are sure.
If we shout, then they will come,
red-cheeked and with bright eyes.

They cross borders
without even knowing:
one day, will be beyond
recall, all trace of them thawed
into valleys, green hills.

# The Children's Encyclopaedia

Good are British soldiers and Jack Cornwell,
Livingstone and Bede and all those born well,
the nurse who speaks good French and helps the boys
by filling up the large trunk with their toys,
good is children with their hair brushed flat
who sit in box-rooms, gazing raptly at
the Stainless Maid of France imploring heaven,
learning that duty is the sinner's leaven.

Jolly is different – mostly foreigners
whose almost English virtue wins them spurs –
but also cavemen who, though knowing little,
clearly meant well with their harmless scribbles.
In rainy weather, jolly means the fun
of cutting paper shapes, or knocking down
a brick upon a table, just like that –
keeping, of course, hands busy, hair brushed flat.

But bad – oh, bad is *schlimm* by definition,
the German War Men and the whiff of gin,
together with those horrid Negro bands,
consumption and the threat of active glands:
worse still, the Devil's child who sees no worth
in Mr Mee's good grammar of the earth –
who dares to speculate on what may lie
beneath the painted gap in Cupid's thighs.

## Post-Operative

Not a cut but a wound
the doctors always called it –
as if wanting to say
that no unkindness was meant,
but also that, besides bleeding,
it would cause hurt too.

Not a cut but a wound –
so that, three years after,
when at night our son sings
bravely to himself for hours,
his mother still sighs and says,
'He is afraid. He remembers.'

And when, rubbing him dry,
I brush the ridge of scar,
I wince and search his eyes
for evidence not of a cut
but a wound that will not heal.
'Shall I sing to you?' I ask.

# Dream Poem

A simple set-up, really: the long black road
leading downhill and, sensed rather than seen,
a single lion ready to run in a furrow
beside the verge. An electric lion, perhaps.

The pace quickens – first mine and then the lion's.
If I run, he runs, and if I choose to affect
a Sunday stroll, he lumbers slackly. I plead
Zeno and fit my feet together in pinsteps.

At the foot of the hill, three nurses in grey and white
pose with a pram on a terrace. I shout a warning,
run for a well-placed door and throw myself in.
Three white faces stare after me, blank as steel.

Logic's no good for dreams: it takes more than Zeno
to match a lion with nannies, wildness with control.
But mostly, from such conjunctions of blood and order,
it's the heart, doctor, the ageing heart which suffers.

# Swimmer Returning

Ahead of me the waves went in
repeating lunar influence
steadily on the beach where stones
clustered like boxed eggs.
Lapped in the wide grooves of the sea
I was all passive, worked upon –
prickled by sunlight, my lips washed
by a dribble of salt, fingers
rubbed loose, wrinkled by water.

Miles of coastline rode at my eyes:
towns with their model frontages
remaindered under hills, high fields
drifting to the edge
of land as simply sliced away
as a piece of cake. And above,
great bluffs of cloud, unmoving floss,
signalled that nothing here could be
the least problematical.

Then, arrival at the shallows
where to swim becomes a pretence:
reluctantly I evolved through
ninety degrees, stood
in abrasive air. I recall
being startled by my own height,
as I shook the sea from my feet
and limped up the sharp slope, each step
now loaded with gravity.

At night I lie flat on my back,
hoisted to high exile above
the city's unending systems.
Half a mile away
the river smacks its concrete lips,
and I dream of the view waiting
at its last turn: the simple sea
waxed by moonlight, the dark dot
of a head bobbed on the waves.

# Old Woman at Threshold

On one hand the hall
where everything is arranged –
a feather of a plant leaning
from a turban of polished brass,
my favourite white gloves ready
as always on the small table
and, by the handrail greased with light,
stairs mounting to darkness.

On the other hand
young grass in its hoop of iron
thriving, buds once more triumphant,
the sundial twisting shadows
round its pointed finger: and then
the privet wall with the square gap
where traffic blurs by, and walkers
always stay in profile.

And I stand between,
balancing on this shrinking ledge,
mad châtelaine of the threshold,
with hair wired tight all round the brain
in which I hear the rising scream
no agency of care or love
can monitor, as the dead weight
of two lost worlds moves in.

## Old Man Exploring

There is no threshold:
the front swings open
entire, revealing
the model of a mind
unhinged to cross-section
at one blow of the knife.

Here in remembrance
no candles are lit:
though the unstarred stems
stand ready, each petite
compartment is its own
dream of dead reckoning.

Nowhere a footfall
or echo, only
immaculate dust
settled on Lilliput,
on its inch-long tables,
its chairs half an inch high.

Somewhere in these cells
lies the point at which
a sense of pattern
overcame the senses:
a room where I may find
sunlight, or rats feasting.

## Changing the Clocks

One hour twice yearly is double or quits
for Doctor Faustus: on the stroke of two
the old régime is toppled in
a bloodless coup.

Prim hands reach up, correcting clock-hands,
and here it comes or goes, the hour
in which the darkest seeds of dreaming
might fully flower.

All sixty minutes stuffed with wishes!
The eleventh hour is tenth or twelfth,
Cinders walks home, or the prince advances
with lustful stealth.

And twice a year we draw back curtains
on light and darkness re-arranged,
see birds above old towers migrating
and time unchanged.

# Chart

The land is a grey hide
wrinkled at the edges
to a shrug of contours
lapsing into grey haze:
even, only perhaps
worth landing to explore.
Inviting departures.

To nose past headlands, split
shoals of swarming numbers!
To nod back at lights fixed
as flicks of pure carmine!
To steer through the flotsam
of words chined by breakers,
m for mud, r for rock...

Far out, the landing-place
floats, serenely anchored,
the compass rose which holds
a fleur-de-lys: not blue,
but still a perfect bloom,
the diagram of all
dreaming immune to storms.

Yet those pale pencil lines
fading into the nap
are also evidence,
telling how ships which haul
seawards all tow the same
thin grey wake, linking them
to ghosts in a grey creek.

# Becalmed

Hulls lollop on the yawning map,
the sails flatly lose their memory,
ropes shrug into trailing loops –
the very idea of allegory
is unbecoming. And yet, and yet
where England blurs, a rough-grained haze,
we think of it as exiles do:
sweet hayricks looming from mists
thick with apples and snatches of Elgar,
the click of slow cartwheels between
green walls in sunken lanes,
a tall trident left leaning
against a burnished oval sun.

Becalmed, we smile idly
across to the strange land,
to the fields of unturned stones.

# The Kingdom of Atlas

## 1

Along the flickering wake
of sunset, the waves glitter
as wickedly tempered as
those cusps of glass which protrude
from the long jaws of my walls.

For this is my rounded realm,
the lethal half-life of fear
enclosed in ring after ring –
the sea hemming the island,
the island warded with walls,
walls which go round the orchards,
orchards which keep the apples,
apples whose cores hold the seeds
of fear, its lethal half-life
enclosed in ring after ring.

The time will come when my words
are all drowned in one echo,
echo which never, never
stops, however quietly,
repeating *the time will come.*

## 2

My herds wander on the hills,
my flocks drink from wide water,
the obedient serpent
hugs the tree, and my children
flourish, their skin soft as milk.

Surely the gods will honour
the maintenance of beauty,
the work of custodians?
I clear the highest gutters
blocked up by the spiteful birds,

I smoke out the deepest mole
at the first lift of the ground.
I am alert to the least
danger, and I know just how
laburnum tempts the children.

But the gods also excel
in irony, who made me
lord of earth's furthermost shores:
possessed, I watch the needy
steal up to my minded doors.


### 3


The world's weight rests on my stem —
lying snug between the skull
and its axis, I support
every shade of opinion,
each gesture of agreement.

I am the fixed point from which
all mapping begins, from where
the lie of the land reveals
its daily experience,
the true value of naming,
the consolations of truth.
Knowing my legend by heart
you will not mistake your path
and may even find in time
the way to welcome strangers.

For this too is my kingdom,
where music may bring down walls
and blossom break from waste ground:
where even now the echo
in your head is a brand-new sound.

## Maze-Walkers
*(in memory of Michael Ayrton)*

They strive above themselves, reading
bodies hemmed in far below as
conventional signs etched upon
a map where green borders enclose
the pilgrim's bull's-eye, intense light.

Progress, they think, needs a mind cool,
cunning for all contingencies:
at this remove no dead end looks
anything more misleading than
the groundplan of an afterthought.

One by one they reach the centre,
pause to confirm success and find
only blankness – and overhead,
cloudbanks coiled in a diffuse glare.


## Hammock Journeys

Inbending,
a hoisted foetus,
you entertain
all possible worlds
except the possible
call from the house;
preferring time,
like disbelief, suspended.

Humming,
you swing, a trophy
bagged and slung
between dark trees
which shoulder you home
through elephant grass;
the English summer
throbs to exotic drums.

Making
great lolling leeway,
your rope canoe
leaks yellow diamonds,
the parasol paddle
trails astern;
sinking, you glimpse
weed on a high blue lake.

Dozing
is vague awareness
of hands being folded,
of the narrow pillow
propping the head,
of coins of light
heavy on eyes;
earth, rich earth is close.

# In the Trout Hatchery

### 1

Superfluous now the upstream gravel
of redds cut clean, the drift of milt:
this river has no story, travels
a table's length, mouths into buckets
and spills away. Sky is a tilt
of dark and starless wood.
Conceived to order, these need no luck.

They harbour their plans. Beneath the skin,
black pips for eyes: each berry stores
enough to last two months of waiting.
As soft as ticks, pre-human, apart,
they glow with knowledge, calmly adoring
the quiet circles of time.
In time, they panic the human heart.

### 2

Black inches spate
beneath the wheel
which regulates
the fall of feed –
a printer's tray
of twitching marks
bumping and turning
through light and dark,
gold-eyed greed.

You gladly shift
your gaze to where
a few fish drift
calmly – one yaws
in rings, its spine
a rigid bend;
eyeless, another
comes to an end
blindly in jaws.

Between two fears
your mind demands
a choice: but here
in one long line
the equal water
shines and shines.

## Dawn Image

I do not even see the face of the bird –
it might be swift, or hobby, or corvine.
There only is a span of stiff, proofed feathers
and the wind's lightning stream which pours
over the lip of the wing's unyielding line.

Across the leading edge it ricochets off
a coat of mail as solid as a plank –
a wind keyed up to long and dark perspectives,
but focussed furiously here,
never to relent till sky is a blue blank.

No hint of destinations either – as if
simple resistance were what mattered most:
as if the proof of it were this stubborn wing
calmly flighting against the light,
high above cities riddled with faceless ghosts.

# The Meat Commission, Kenya

Beached upcountry
it rides the hills,
all cabins lit,
a frantic steamer
waving the flag
of its fine name.

Daily the cattle
replenish the ark,
nodding to their death
in a shroud of dust,
fruit of the plain's
long seasons.

And daily the knife
divides and discards:
horn and hoof
rattle down chutes,
tinned flesh
glints in the railyards.

In how many places
with fine names
have sleeves been rolled
above blood level,
even in the name
of our salvation?

Night and day
the maribous wait
and, trembling, adore
the curdled air.
Their endless appetites
burden the trees.

# Fire Raiser

Trees and hayricks,
houses and stables,
all have danced for me
in their true shape,
and all have yielded
the same swart image
of my father naked,
purged of opinions,
speechless in the flames'
universal tongues.

The smallest stick-fire
melts to a core
of model truth
in that mad eyeblink
when frameworks collapse,
when creation flares
beyond its inheritance
to Pentecost roses,
purest neutralities,
my dancing flowers!

Only, waking
in darkness to find
over charred chevrons
the sky in its coldness
unregenerate,
again I fear
my father undead
in the soft ash
and pray for a dawn
silent, with no bird rising.

# Roses Climbing

What are they to do with love,
the high roses looping above the trellis?
No hand has ever held their buds
like a wine-glass between its fingers
to sip the perfume, or admire
the contours of a heartland free of faults.

Look – just here and again, here,
a few timely cuts would have curbed their climbing
and made a shapely bush whose flowers
hands or lips could stroke at their pleasure:
on summer nights the air would be
hung thick with sweetness rising from below.

These, untrained, grow wild in sky
on stems gross and wickedly barbed with purple:
for weeks they wag to the high winds
then explode in a fount of petals,
cascade to earth. And you will know,
my love, how truth demands I leave them so.

# The Drinking Songs of Attila

### 1

What makes a city?
The stink of defeated nomads.
What makes a borough?
Saddles cracked with age.
What makes a township?
Women's voices blockading
thresholds with their patient rage.

What makes a suburb?
Tents frozen into gables.
What makes a ghetto?
Power in the wrong hands.
What makes a village?
Brittle ploughshares, dividing
acres of divided land.

What makes for freedom?
Ah, the answer to that,
my feckless burghers,
is hidden somewhere between
my hollow cheek
and your rictus grins.

### 2

I give you deserted garage forecourts
and the endless grammar of grey crescents.
I give you double glazing, and miles
of regular religious hedges.
I give you the last recorded minutes
of the last committee to be impaled
on points of order with a cutting edge:
drink with me to their open options!

Think of the mannered groves of learning
stiff with gas, the faculties
besieged by panic. Think of the children
penning their sour memoirs in words
they scribble on graveyard walls. Think
of the Legion of the Lark, on the east border,
unpaid for months, still oiling their swords:
drink with me to their open options!


3

I drink to the homage of Hollywood,
to fables bright as a Chinese parrot –
Attila the baddie, Attila the good –
to the propaganda of brazen trumpets
calling the armies once again
to conflicts easily understood –
Attila the monk plays Attila the hood.

Gentlemen, is it too late
to remember those who survived?
Is it not thanks to me
that Venice came to rise
on the shores of a tame sea?
My scarlet music was wiser
than any guarded gate.


4

Remember also the Danube as it was
on the day of my wedding and of my death –
cusps of brightness riding the flow,
the mist drifting like a slow breath...
Bullshit! I've often turned my back
on more exquisite gloom than that.
I give you instead the god I made
in your own image: the settling dregs
of all my golden hero's dreams.

# The Auction Rooms

Daily, in the undertaker's clearing-house,
money is nodded away in vague exchange
for sleepwalkers' bargains, the crazy household
of job lots quite impervious to fashion.
Here in the last redoubt of manufacture
outrageous curiosity can redeem
anything wheeled out of a burning city
or lacking appeal to cool inheritors.

In time, almost everything goes: but never
bedlinen. Never that – a single night's use
seems infection enough. Month on month it grows,
a hill rusted with iron-mould, a pale taboo
whose stiff slopes of Turin microfilm enfold
the privately printed history of death.

# Five Thoughts of the Violinist

### 1

Proudly I jut across the lights,
the violin and its eighty-four parts
pouched between chin and shoulder-blade.
We fit exactly: my right arm,
double-jointed, is tipped with pearl.
Down tracks of gut and steel I sight
my left hand scrolled to match the wood.

But here he comes – my *alter ego*,
the fearsome cripple who, each night,
repacks his weathered limbs in velvet
and falters down the city tunnels:
a busker bundled off his pitch
with nothing but a wavering echo
to see him to the end of darkness.

### 2

Before a note is played
solo I orchestrate
the separate components:
metal hauled to daylight,
*spiccato* horses springing
up to a bar-line fence,
pink sponges of sheep
dabbed along cropped slopes –
and from air the dense
solidity of maple.
Easy as bird I bracket
a sunlit congruence –
every level homing,
declining in a cadence.

3

It comes to this, a wall put up between
expectant hush and that resounding moment
before the clapping: a way to separate
two almost silences.
                              Within the first
I hear, like sea-noise sounding in a shell,
a chisel worrying at a stub of wood,
the tiny flick of shavings as they land
in curlicues beneath the craftsman's bench.
The air vibrates with rough and rhythmic hands
which polish smooth.
                              It is perhaps his children
who scatter, laughing, when the music's finished.
Somewhere over the wall, their voices whisper
then vanish in a hailstorm of applause.


4

*A small and narrow study, having*
*one window: a thin partition*
*dividing off the noisy schoolroom.*
*Outside, a nearby mill-wheel clanking.*
But nothing was too hard for Bach –
dishonest clerks, insomniac counts,
the family deaths – through all of these
he kept on east, from Eisenach
to rising light. Poking from lace,
those massive fists outreached all ills,
rebuilding out of noise and rubble
elaborations to a quiet end.


5

sous le pont
du violon
four fingers
tap-dance on
the blackened board.

I am the king
of dissolutions,
the perfect hybrid
of other lives
bolted together,
drunkenly watching
my borders blur
under a rain
as fine as rosin.

# Poem for a Cinema Organist

Fifteen years ago you sank
in glorious bars of purple light,
your silver hair
a landmark where
an era disappeared from sight.

Now, as unpredictably,
you surface here, inside a school,
to intercede
in sloppy tweeds
for all things bright and beautiful.

Metronomic fingers wag
around the old harmonium –
when pleasure's gone
God's antiphon
is what the prodigal becomes.

God be praised, at your first touch
usherettes tap-dance down the aisles,
improving quatrains
melt to profane
Savoy arpeggios, wicked style.

Sparkling syncopations guard
the faith you've kept while growing older –
while angels hum
the rainbow comes
to curve its colours at your shoulder.

# The Kite-Tail
*(for Richard Swarbrick)*


Full of breath it persists,
a cursive script composed
on unlined paper, gestures
of florid loops, the wrist
turned over and over –
repeating victory-rolls
in honour of style, even
when only a miracle
could save the kite from falling.

And when, winded at last,
the frail cross-trees lie
flapping on curt moor-grass,
here comes yard after yard
of spiralling blue, shaping
the last arpeggio trilled
on the sinking liner's decks –
one bright blue kite-tail writing
the history of bravado.

## At Rye
*(for Patric Dickinson)*


The facts are brilliantly alleged –
famous residents, antique streets,
the glaze of earthenware – and all
infer the statute hoisted above
the church: *for our time is a very shadow*
*that passeth away.* Flanking the text,
the quarterboys smirk in their gilt fat.

And two miles south, a plausible sea
unwinds as it should onto a beach
of shells milled to shards of bone.
Where neaps and springs quarter the days,
shifting their mane of sticky kelp
across the shore, who could contest
the evidence of time passing?

Appearances smooth as an alibi –
But here at the town's brink, the cliff
insists on posing for the perfect cadence
only water could hope to complete.
Within its shadow, houses and meadows
laid in the wake of the absent sea
are inadmissible, pure illusion.

Into that zone no facts can cover,
real as the oldest hopes of love
or the sag left in my father's chair,
the ocean floods back, beating like blood,
proof against time. At night I feel it
lapping at my mind, where the quiet triumphs
of the dead are borne in on a rising tide.

## Eating Maize

From the very first it has been
a history of destructions:
the long leaves wincing,
silky tassels torn away
from buttery knuckles clenched
as tightly as a grenade.

Year after year I suck
the sweet and yellowed bone
of rich summer, teeth
burrowing inwards until
the racks are hollow, and I hold
nothing but tough litter.

Then I dream how with one
long and careful cut
I might find, inside the core,
a whole hillside crackling
with head-high plantations,
acres of solid fruit.

Supreme illusionist,
I can recreate hope
endlessly, like a set
of gleaming Russian dolls
by Caesarian section
out of a single season.

Yet from the first it was
a history of destructions:
in winter I see myself
as an old but never replete
cannibal, eating my heart out
with a terrible hunger for innocence.

# South Yorkshire

Transactions seethe from cooling-towers
deep in submissive meadows wormed
with stopcocks, fine filters, bolted pipes.
Fat reservoirs of old habits,
like dazed relics the cattle confront
light retreating to a raw line
along canals. On every side
strictest codes enjoin the landscape.

To each village its gothic dogma,
the low skyline buttressed at pits·
with black lattices, wheels which decline
day and night in a flick of spokes.
To each mine its ragged pentecost
of flame held high into the wind,
proclaiming from lips greasy with soot
that work is love, a sacred cow.

But canny, orthodox old women
keep to their cramped parlours, obsessed
with cleanliness, and not forgetting
their younger selves already bent
double all the day long, collecting
tatties to earn a beggar's wage:
still they wonder at the pure paleness
of those nuggets prised from dark soil.

They take for emblem the turned thumbful
of white oilpaint gleaming above
the power-plant stack: that, at their death,
they too may rise, a clean harvest
hatched from the diocese of dust –
in dreams, seeing how their clear blood
might blossom from broken pipes to bless
the fields, revoke all heresies.

## Shells

Along the banded beach
lie tellins, bright crash-landed butterflies,
with shells of mussels, blue and glossy almonds,
and scallops, fossil fans laid out to dry.
Shells, like words, are what you make of them –
pilgrims' badges, money, pubic shields,
Aztec tribute, scoops for holding oil,
pastry moulds or gems.

To match the shining fragments
or find the metaphor of a different use
appears retrieval of a kind, but brings
no sense of shape: the bits remain diffuse
as waves are in the sparkling air of distance.
Beneath the minded phrases, what remains
is half a story, lifeless beauty shrugged
off by tides, a clearance.

Imagination learns
to work at absences, to re-invent
the valves of stranded swimmers, burrowers, borers,
their slimy hearts, their palps and ligaments –
and only then may hope to see, salt-fresh,
the ocean purling tamely at her heels,
Aphrodite as she is, a resurrection
not of words but flesh.

FROM **DEVOTIONS**

(1987)

# Snooker Players

They whistle the fine smoke
Of blue dust from the cue,
Suave as gunslingers, never
Twitching one muscle too few.
At ease, holstering their thumbs
In trimmest waistcoats, they await
Their opponent's slip, the easiest
of shots miscalculated.
Their sleek heads shine, spangled
With the sure knowledge of every angle.

Once at the table, they bend
In level reverence to squint
At globe after globe, each
With its window of light glinting
On cushioned greener than green,
The rounded image of reason.
One click and cosmology thrives,
All colours know their seasons
And tenderly God in white gloves
Retrieves each fallen planet with love.

Watching them, who could believe
In the world's lack of balance?
Tucked in this pocket of light
Everything seems to make sense –
Where grace is an endless break
And justice, skill repaid,
And all eclipses are merely
A heavenly snooker displayed.
Yet all around, in the framing
Darkness, doubt dogs the game.

## Allotments

*(for Charles Causley)*


Since time continues to demand its bleak honours,
let them be awarded here, where thrift cuts wastage
to a minimum – old elixirs corked with rag
in sheds as close and devotional as chantries –
where each new year the gaudy seed-packets signal
the resurrection of hope, and by grass duckboards
the twine unwinds to love in its fruiting season.

The allotments have become their own aerial view –
the land as it appears in the gunner's reticle,
squared into simple plots, as a god might see it,
familiar yet strange, the workings of creatures
who seem to believe, but almost as a hobby:
and always the same workings, set at the edges
of every railway journey and of dark canals.

Even the ornaments recur – the upturned bowls
riddled with couch-grass, or the bicycles leaning
at a post, or the smoke rising in unison
from autumn fires, or the clack of spades resounding,
or the soft shifting of sieves. Here time will run out
endlessly, but can never defeat the tenants
of the last real estate of common prayer.

# At Possenhofen
*(for John Mole)*


The meadow in its mildness stretches on
And on beside the waters of the lake
Whose shallows, cloudy as kaolin, support
Boat after boat saluting to the breeze.

Games are played, bright frisbees slice the air,
Children run about, fall and get up again.
Blue smoke drifts by from meat being burnt.
People are idly kissing and talking and jigging
Up and down by rubber dugouts, blowing
With their feet; or lying pegged out on little jetties
Which sacrifice them to the fiery summer sun.
Many also are swimming, close to some swans.

They have discovered an African freedom from scale,
Each has escaped to become a function of all –
All the brown bodies, the simple vanities
Of dark brown breasts and the swanky male bulge,
Or the strip of bikini swooping down between legs
To grip the minimal groin and shout, like that one
There, in fluorescent green, 'Look at my tan!' –
A whole species on holiday from hermeneutics!

As if history had no value but accretion,
Were really just a mad king or two building castles
In Spain or Bavaria, then quietly drowning
Each in his own dark lake. But every garden
Of earthly delights will conjure the triumph of death:
Beyond the wood, the railway runs straight past
Brueghel's Spanish soldiery to soul's north,
That other nakedness, those other fires.

In today's breeze, boat after boat nods:
Beside the lake the meadow stretches on
South of Dachau. Here nobody sees more
Than what they see. No one mentions God.

# Reichert's Leap

*(In December 1911, Walter Reichert, a self-employed
tailor, attempted to fly from the Eiffel Tower)*

Each hopeless stitch homemade – the futile skin
Out of which he would jump. It's too late now,
Even if he wanted, as surely he must be wanting,
To climb down. He crouches on the cold brow
Of madness, on the parapet's fine brink,
His breath smearing the air, an unused silence
Which might have been saving speech. *Here, what do you think?*
*I didn't mean it. Of course. It makes no sense.*
Or simply, *We'll have a drink and then I'll go*
*To embrace my poor wife and children. Later, we'll chat.*
Too late. They say the journalists wouldn't throw
Their story out of the window, and that was that.
He shifts like a bird – ridiculous, he fears.
*Go on, you're chicken.* He cannot, will not stay
For this. A puff of looping breath. The sheer
Drop. The stupid tower begins to sway
In his mind only. A final shuffle and
A plop as into water. The deficient air
Fails to support him. A black duster lands,
Bundles into the ground. A brief affair.
Men in caps. Fuss. A canvas shroud.
A way elbowed through the encroaching crowd.

Which of us, from our tower, would not recall
This brute parabola of pride and fall? –
Late Romantics, fledgling birdmen all.


# Boatman Shot

Reading it in the paper, it seemed quite simple –
*The Times* correspondent, coming to a lake
In northern El Salvador, had wanted to cross
With five other newsmen, in order to discover
Whether the army, American-trained, had killed
Some peasants in land the guerrillas controlled. Old story.

San Nicolás, the hamlet in the story,
Was just that, its people plain and simple –
As was the evidence that the army had killed
Possibly more than a hundred. Back on the lake
The boat sank, leaving the travellers to discover
Their own way home, with a day's jungle to cross.

Back in San Salvador, in the shadow of the cross,
The boatman tasted whisky, went the story,
For the first time ever, and was happy to discover
What kept the newsmen going. He found it simple –
Just as it had been to ferry them over the lake
And find the villagers whom the soldiers had killed.

Two days after, the National Guard, who killed
For a living, came and took the boatman to cross-
Examine him about the foreigners at the lake
And about his part in a bad news story
Implying abuse of human rights. It was simple –
The truth, they said, was all they wanted to discover.

Finally they released him, unable to discover
The truth of what had happened, or who had killed
The villagers. The boatman, back in his simple
House, began to realise that to cross
From one shore to another was a story
Which had its hidden depths, just like the lake.

Too late he glimpsed the figures rising from the lake,
Some dressed like soldiers, in green. They did not discover
Anything worth listening to in his story.
They took the boatman out of his house and killed
Him then and there. His widow bears the cross
Of seven children. The future looks very simple.

Suchitlan was the lake, Alas the boatman killed.
This poem is his, who discovered and ferried across
The necessary truth, keeping the story simple.

# African Moments

### 1

What the sun most brightly shines on
is not the Presidential Suite
not the Hotel Continental
not the cinema's cool plush depths
not the taxidermist's trophies
not the straw of packing-cases
not the traffic lights and meters
not the haze of the loud bazaar
but the puddle bright as tin
beneath the slum's one public tap
from which water slowly dripping
discharges all the wanton seeds
of hope which ride inside the belly
of every Trojan horse of a city.

### 2

Our host, apologetic, indicates
wood and canvas buckled on the verandah,
a torn rainbow of colours, with stiff limbs
wrecked at all angles – and, tight-lipped, explains,
'Damned hyenas, at the deck-chairs again.'

Later, when the boy has cleared and gone,
he sighs a little, adding that he thinks
all history is really very simple.
Enter the tyrants, shouldering deck-chairs:
the people howl with laughter in their lairs.

# Goodbyes
*(for Erica)*


From behind the door, a toe
waggled at knee height –
or an arm, or a head. As she goes
she comes back, or bits of her do,
like a party game which might
find room for mad Carew.

At ten she already seems
privy to the dark spell
of loss, the impossible dream
of love's impossible sorrows –
and can break it by saying farewells
over the head of tomorrow.

'Goodbye, goodbye – I've gone!'
Once more, the head. 'I'm still
here!' Her feet drum on
the stairs. Then, above,
a slowly receding drill –
the bodied echo of love.

## Runners, Fading
*(for Matthew)*

How long ago was it
when they broke from the line
at crazy speed, urged on
by the fear of not fitting
that first hedge-gap?

Before the race, waiting,
they had looked pitiful,
much too clumsy, their legs
too gawky, the black numbers
pinned on askew.

Standing, sucking their breath
and ignoring ahead,
they let their feet stutter
on wet grass. One or two tried
to tell a joke.

Then they were off, upping
and downing and jostling,
slowly spreading, starting
to move less up and down, more
smoothly along.

They have gone now, fading
into distance like a
new dimension, beyond
recognition: and we wait
as if for forgiveness.

Slumped, an obvious parent,
inside the steamed-up car,
I long to hear the plimp
of feet on tarmac: to see
you, returning.

# Dreaming of My Father

Up and up together we went
Through the rich, narrow garden,
Me and my father. A steep ascent
And the stairs of grass were hard,
Filled in. He was leaving at last.
*Ja, ja, die Treppe*, he murmured,
Smiling, recalling the interred
Treads of the hollow past.

As we climbed, he began to reveal
The names of flowers: once he paused
To admire the progress of seeds sealed
In candy-stripe drinking-straws.
Twice, softly, he spoke my name –
But each time he did so, I heard
The voice of my stepmother – an absurd
Acoustic trick, I thought, or a game.

I looked at him, then realised:
This time *he* had lived longer.
Although he looked very tired, his eyes
Were just as blue as when, much younger,
He had ridden a donkey right through Crete,
His jacket loose about his shoulders,
Self-consciously handsome, and so bold
He had looked almost immune to defeat.

And now, gently, he was reciting
The names of all the plants that stood
In a warm hutch, the last on the right,
On a long shelf of wood.
They grew on dolls'-house teapots
Whose lids were turned upside-down –
And every single one
Was a kind of forget-me-not.

# A Tooth

The bottom edges thin to a frill of bone,
Its top is a scrimshaw carved with a dream of home:
Inside, something secret – between dried bits of red,
A hollow D. And it gleams richly, like a stone
Enamelled by water washing over the river-bed.

How it calls for a socket, for a marching jaw,
For a full house snugly set! Yet is no talisman,
No white cliff waving its emblems to tearful exiles,
No headstone memory, not even a shallow store
For the fossil fragments of a lost childhood smile.

Only, once it was not, so that what it enfolds
Is a journey to death, but also a journey to life –
As if a single fleck of sperm had frozen
Solid and grown, right on the womb's threshold,
Prelude and aftermath equally blank, unchosen.

It is nothing more, though, than a flake of bone, a gap
Which will not last, the merest whistle in a word,
A single blob of rain lost in a lake,
Done without, discarded: and still it traps
The heart, demanding a status greater than keepsake.

I weigh it now in my hand – gingerly, lest
A jolt should send it rolling between the boards
Or into a dusty corner, to be lost for ever –
Shapeless as spilt milk, but for ever impressed
With the image of a daughter calmly asleep, who never

Wakes when someone slips a cold coin under
Her pillow, or complains about the taste
Of blood, old and metallic, infecting her dreams.
I try not to notice the time, or even to wonder
At how dark on the white bed-linen her fair head seems.

# Ring

As casually as passing the salt
You handed me your wedding ring to keep –
Such savour! Such half-witting balancing out!
And I was the star-struck native, exalted
Beyond reason by the curio, wondering how
It might have removed my soul in my sleep.

The names it bore had been inscribed
Fifty years before: years that have streamed
Wildly through its hoop and gone to air.
I think of its usage – the constant sliding
On and off, the warp of wear and tear,
A pledge less and less redeemed.

Through it, as lightly as a kiss
To a sleeping child, once the two of you blew
The South Sea Bubble of love's brief monsoon –
What I hold now is your shining vocative
Long since reduced to zero, the punched moon
Haunting the forest's dying avenues.

Perhaps if I held it up to my eye
I might see my father on a rare visit, bending
To kiss your hand: or, putting it to my ear,
Would hear him laughing to the point of crying –
Or you saying, as you often do, *The war
Had a lot to do with the marriage ending.*

At my father's grave, the wind flicks
Through unkempt grass. You often stay up late
And wake early. And I am the star-struck native,
Unborn again, dazzled by a golden cervix,
Emblem of the gift that the two of you have given,
Worth every ounce of its weight.

# An Incident in Kent

*(for Elinor Moore)*


My daughter, at six, almost drowned
At a swimming pool in Kent, at a school.
It was nobody's fault – she had been in already,
Had dressed and returned and was bending down
To splash a friend who was still in the pool
When suddenly in she went, head

Over heels. As quickly the friend dived
To get her. That was all. Soon after,
She learned to swim. For her, what stays
Vivid is not the shock of revival
But two boys and their unkind laughter
At seeing her baptised, buried and raised.

For me, what stays is what she said
At the the time, hardly retrieved, gasping:
*I knew I was safe because I could see*
*The water there above my head.*
Words that might have been her last ·
Or locked in her throat for eternity –

And I think of Hugo at Soubise, sitting down
In a café with his mistress, ordering beer
And opening a paper without any foreboding
To read of his daughter's death by drowning –
*His face and his hair were wet with tears.*
*His poor hand was pressed to his heart as though...*

The rest of the story could hardly mean
More than post-mortem – the early mist,
The lightness of the dinghy, which made them ship
Two stones as ballast: Léopoldine
Changing her mind, unable to resist
Her husband's smile or the thought of the trip.

At Caudebec, yet more stones
To reassure cautious Maître Bazire,
The lawyer. Then, after a lull,
A sudden gust. All the weight thrown
To one side. Capsize. No help near.
Didine clinging for a time to the hull...

The mother sat, fingering strands
Of the drowned girl's hair, hour after hour.
She kept her red-checked dress to dote on,
Folded in a bag. With trembling hand,
*I loved that poor child beyond my power
To express in words*, the poet wrote.

What else could he write, but that the grass
Must grow, and children die – what do,
But volley the blanks of guilt and grief
At a God who had fallen to black farce?
What words, what art could see him through
To any believable kind of belief?

He could not help himself: each year
He wrote a poem for the rose-planted grave,
Phrase after phrase still keenly edged –
Till somehow he re-invented the world
Of love, by imagining being there: saved
By seeing the water above his head.

# Fable

He found a stone shaped like a heart
On a rattling beach, in the last spring
His parents shared. It needed no art,
Felt heavy, had good colouring,
Would pass for real, or once real, rather.
Smiling, he gave it to his father.

That summer she found a stone like a hand
In a stream, and on it painted a sleeve,
Black buttons, a white cuff and
One accusing finger leaving
No room for doubt, or little, rather.
She thought it would amuse her father.

Their father built a house of stones
Which, polished and angled, could skim the light
In rooms where now he lived alone.
Perhaps the children thought to write,
Perhaps he, with his hand on his heart,
Would swear he could feel the haemhorrhage starting.

# Hallowe'en Lantern

In the darkness, a face, skull-nosed,
Saw-toothed, slit-eyed – each year
A child's wild one-man show
Of root savagery would glow
At the window, in a rough blur.

Its soft brain, very neatly
Gouged, spooned clean away,
Had left its crass top completely
Ill-fitting, a soup-pot where sweetly
The smell of burning stayed.

Crackling waxily, profane,
Neckless, a drunken dome,
It stood between curtain and pane
Facing the frost or the dark rain
Through which I shivered home.

My mind's a blank. What went on
Behind that grin, in those banging
Rooms which belong to no one?
My children will go, my wife has gone –
In the darkness I see a face, hanging.

# Rain on Roses

The house was sold four years ago, but still
It comes to haunt me, that soft image of rain,
Those oily, pudgy globules that would not spill
Down from the fine-toothed leaves, simply staying.
Shining with light, that knowledge which arrives
To drench the already drenched, those raindrops seemed
On guard, warding me off lest I should try
To penetrate the green leaves' shadowy dreams.

Were there, then, other secrets to be uncovered
By greater strength, by scattering what lay
Across the threshold – or was it just that love
Must sometimes guard its secrets to win the day?
I see those rosebuds kissing into air and throwing
The raindrops off, and still I do not know.


# Diastole, Systole

The heart is a window looking out
Onto a garden where all paths lead
Through past winters and future springs
Into the summer, drowning doubt
In hazy ease. Here, each seed
Fruits to the fullest bloom of being,
Knowing its end from the greenest start,
Aware that giving is a dying art.

The heart is a window looking in
Onto a room where all our past lives
Darken to sweet and painful shadows,
The time-locked womb where hope must begin
To recognise itself and thrive
If lover is ever to attain the rose –
The rose, my love, whose heart may yet distil
True fragrance, and leave the summer air fulfilled.

# Rocamadour

What light concealed, the darkness brings to light:
Seventy times seven, the human urges
Ranked in melting turrets, the wavering verges
Stacked in hope against the soul's dark night.

A fakir's bed of nails, on which to lay
An antidote to fear or to regret:
*I wish, I wish* – each tallow pronoun sweats
Its limited plea into the iron tray.

Across the walls, the proof in solid stone,
A gallery of favours, faith rewarded:
Row after row of triumph, thanks recorded
To the Black Virgin, who sits upon her throne

With Jesus perched on the edge of her left knee.
Angular, rigid, candle-flames catching the lights
In her crown – her eyes turned inward, blank as night,
Demanding everything, blind with certainty.

I lit a candle, too, and followed you out,
Hoping you had not seen. *Oh please, oh please* –
Clean as the mouth of a tunnel, that doorway cleaving
The darkness of faith and the pale day of doubt.

# The Quarry at Haytor

Each numb bud
held in a vice,
locked beyond echo
in its chamber of ice:

and the waterfall solid,
clipped to the sill
of the high scarp,
acutely still.

In the pent silence
we made birds sing,
shared the pulse
of water quickening:

and as we watched,
by our warm power
the soft-fleshed trees
burst into flower.

Later, autumn
rusted the heather
and the bright fern lay
like scattered feathers:

where the water fell
two lilies turned
and turned, forlorn
in a dark cistern.

Through the bullying wind
I heard you call,
faithful and fearful,
somehow appalled:

and looking back
I saw summer and spring,
the half-worked veins
still shining, shining.

# English Versions

This is the English year's translation of sorrow –
A failed late May, in which tense families walk
Through dripping avenues of rhododendrons
Where rain has washed the flowers to mortal paleness.
Hearts ache by the dark, peaty lake, its surface
More wrinkled than a prune.

No horizon looks through into tomorrow,
but somewhere a smooth political voice keeps talking –
'Spend! Spend! Spend!' It bleakly booms, intent on
Drowning despair. In a flapping marquee, for sale,
Dogged home produce, damp books. A draw takes place
For remaindered June.

And here is the English calendar's rendering of bliss –
The uncut grass of wildly catholic meadows
Stained blue and red, beneath the massy heights
Of candled chestnuts: a sweetness of May air
That only lovers could hope to multiply
In naked heat.

Nothing conceivably could be added to this:
Faith is a static heat-haze, neither to nor fro,
Simple as the switchback lanes hemmed in so lightly
By cloudy drifts of cow-parsley. Overhead, somewhere,
June begins in a far calm lake of sky
Where sun and moon meet.

# Cricket Scoreboard

*(for Hubert Moore)*


History only begins
Outside, at the slits hacked
In the cereal packet, like a peepshow,
By a child on a wet day.
In their sharp morse the scorers
Claim every action for fact:
Yet here in the hutch's dark glow,
In the gloaming of grass-smell and resin,
All possible matches are played.

But for darkness and rain
Such heat would surely prove
Too rich, and the great sums set
In white, too bright a demonstration
Of time's endless curve. The canvas
On the warped rollers hardly moves:
By the loops of numbers boys sweat
The seasons away, yet remain
Fiercely devoted to their stations.

Meanwhile, out in the field
Whole careers go missing,
Fading in the breeze to a hum
Of bar-time conversations.
Team after team shakes down
To almanach averages – but this
Stays fresh through countless summers:
The sweet-smelling box which shields
Dark and triumphant declarations.

# Boxers

Between these twanging staves
Is only the bell's one-two –
Clock, Farewell or Surprise,
The crowd's cheers or boos.

Above the glossy shorts
They've only the silk of sweat
And the blank grin that tries
To camouflage pain and regret.

They must keep dancing, keep
Those kidneys, cherry-red,
On the attack, or begging
Close into the head.

They must keep dancing, must
Avoid those double figures –
But such directness, in time,
Will take its toll of vigour:

Like passionate lovers they
Will tangle in the end,
And gently be eased apart
By their natty mutual friend.

Yet they allow those men
In the corners to give them stick
Till they wince, to sponge them, send them
Back to face the music.

Long before it's over
They want an end to harm,
To fall, *ponderoso*,
Into each other's arms.

But blood is blood and, besides,
They can hear through the smoky din
That voice which is always waiting
On the far side of any win:

*You're only just as good, son,*
*As you are in your next bout –*
Darkness and common time,
And the bell ringing down and out.


## Two Figures


Dart is deaf and digs the garden strip:
He wears blue trousers with a slick city stripe.
With them manacled to his legs he reaches the house
On a clicking bicycle heavy as any horse.
He wields the pump as if he wants to knock
The stuffing out of you. He also may take knick-knacks
That take his eye. Sometimes he asks to be fired.
Once he hurled a brick at our hired black Ford.
He talks to himself and seems to be quite at home.
His wife, seen once, is somehow part of him –
In curlers, with funny eyes and very short,
And a floral apron over a man's shirt.

And Membury the dwarf who lives just short
Of the thundering trains which every so often shoot
Smoke from the cutting up in a ragged fan –
Membury yellow as the *Beano* and *Radio Fun*
In his front window, who really wears gaiters and hoards
All his money in a large tin box which he hides.
His darkened parlour smells equally of cats,
Newsprint and pee. Not even *Comic Cuts*
Has anyone to beat him. His piping voice,
Absurdly shrill, seems caught in some mad vice:
He tries and tries to clear his little throat,
Nervous as a lizard, as if afraid of threats.

Both long dead – but here they come, unhurried,
The dark grotesques of vivid childhood fears,
Spotless in detail, arcing over the years,
Harbingers of all not dead, just buried.

# A Birthday Portrait

If I were painting you, I would ask you to sit
Here, against the trunk of the large horse chestnut –
In May, of course, with the vivid fan of green,
Ribbed and vaulted, enormously flicked open
In peacock display, the brightest royal flush
Of spring's matchless suit.

At your back, inviolable strength,
Ancient authority sucked once more into shadow –
Here all systems seem inward, each tongue of leaf
Has a trunk and branches, each single tree
Builds its own fleshy forests of pink and white
Rising in soft pagodas.

Underfoot, the ground is wormed by roots,
The delved earth sifted to a powder finer
Than hourglass grains. Overhead, long weathers
Express themselves in shifting syncopations
Of sound and silence, the sun's dark humming heat,
The moon's pale knowledge.

I would have only to watch you, as you sat
At the still hub, as you watched the fields turn,
The landscape make loving sense, although you know
That hope is always deciduous, and hearts
Not always trumps…When you began to smile,
Then I would start to paint.

# A Compliment to Pissarro
*(for Georgie)*


I have never been to Eragny and yet
It always seems to advance, slanting slightly,
To meet or greet me, spreading the long shadows
Of its trees and buildings across the evening sunlight.

I know its church, that spire's fine secret point
Escaping from ambushing trees. And those cows in the field –
If I had to, I could call all four by their names,
Just as I could the locals. Ask Mathilde.

I know which shutters creak, and how the barn
Must baffle the wind and harbour the hot hay;
And what the drenching moonlight might discover
Deep in the silent houses, where every day

Drifts to the grainy air of summer dusk
And the easy hours of two lying close, the lace
Curtain barely lifting to purple sky...
Of the artist and his easel, not a trace.

## Nude Coming Downstairs
*(after Duchamp)*


I am not this one or that one,
here or now, then or when –
I am a multiple negative,
Never cancelling myself,
Not going upstairs.

I am not anything as simple
As the central figure: I've tried.
Even my sex is unclear,
I am so clad in movement,
So decently blurred.

For all I know, we might have
Stepped clean off the roundabout
Somewhere between maybe
And has-been, but forgetting nothing,
Expecting everything still.

One of us has to decide
What to do when we reach
The hall: how best to greet
Anyone who might be waiting
With flowers for me, for me.

# Mr and Mrs Campbell

*(for Jimmy and Margie)*


For nineteen years, two continents and five countries
Your houses have been for me a style as concise
    As well packed cases, a shorthand plural
        For what you value most.

I agree that in part it's a matter of pretty *objets* –
The stones you polish and, even though you possess
    Any number, can proudly name, or the silver
        From Ethiopia, or the rugs –

But emblems too: in an earlier age you might have
Been given the credit for first bringing marrows to Rome,
    Or sunflowers to Kenya, or both to Belgium.
        Nor should the world forget

The encouragement given such plants in quite other places,
Like Oundle and Kent. And besides, wherever you've lived,
    Paper globes have always flourished – and
        Light and lightness of touch.

Yet when I picture you, what comes to mind is never
Such travellers' constants papering over the gaps,
    But stillness – as if an artist had caught you
        Calmly at ease against

A landscape to which you belong and have belonged always,
Like Mr and Mrs Andrews on rich home ground –
    Defined not by walls, or even by being
        English or open to the sky,

But simply by being the place where your friends and journeys
Pass through, where you faithfully sow, water the plants
    And share the same love and lightness, always:
        May you not ever move.

# The Cemetery at Gufidaun

The years flow in and out of the trees,
Neap and summer, winter and spring,
The same slow mulch as the sea.

The starboard lights are steady in the lee
Of the headstones, where the dead are lying
Straight as any tree.

Dressed in their best, they seem to be
In mourning for themselves. You can hear a sighing
Just like the heaving sea.

Over the green waves longingly
Glide their regrets like a great bird flying
Into the rigging of the trees.

Silence, then, or the monody
Of the iron bell in the spire crying
Like a buoy at sea,

Bitter and hard as eternity
Under the cold, bright stars in the sky.
The years flow in and out of the trees,
The same slow mulch as the sea.

## Christmas Night

On the wind, a drifting echo
of simple songs. In the city
the streetlamps, haloed innocents,
click into instant sleep.
The darkness at last breathes.

In dreams of wholeness, irony
Is a train melting to distance;
and the word, a delighted child
gazing in safety at
a star solid as flesh.

# Shrine

At the crossed feet sprang roses, blood-red
On thorny stems: in the up-ended
Coffin of pain, someone had hooked
A maize cob onto each nailed palm.
Two long, blackening lobes, they looked
Ridiculous, pagan. And twice more
On the same road, this clumsy semaphore
Dangled from the outstretched arms.

Arms still as the trickled blood
That the artist had let dribble from the rood
Down over limbs of painted plaster –
Yet what, in time, most comes across
Is not that god of triumphant disaster
But mortal fruit, the flesh that yields
To time; and over the blackened fields,
The roses' shining gloss.

# Apologia

Such riddling quiddities, such suppositions!
Men say that Christ at least was in the world,
Even if not of it; while we have turned
Our backs, in order to practise our devotions –
A narrow virtue barely squeezed between
Addiction and indulgence. Do they think
I twitch blindly through from matins and lauds
To compline and the silence? I know as well
As any man which army's where, or how
To bind a beggar's sores, or what is meant
By swelling in the groin, or gobs of blood.

Lately I did the Psalms – and still like best
The first – the blessing in *Beatus* given
In stem and branch, a pair of crouching lions,
Birds and a cat's mask, the whole most richly done
With vine and oak leaves, brightened with acanthus.
Now, it's the Gospels: on a ground of green,
Light blue and lavender, the drops of gold
Lifted with care across the smooth, ruled vellum.
L for Matthew, already done, then I
For Mark, Q for Luke, then I again
For John – red ivy, with columbine, I think...

I do not pretend, as the truly ruthless do,
That any pain can be contracted to fit
The fluency of words or shining paint –
Or that the world's my cloister. All my art,
Beneath rich foliage, curling metaphor,
Commutes between God's world and the Trappist heart.
Yet what is learned in silence needs its say –
Next year, if I am spared, I hope to start
On a new challenge, my first Book of Hours.
I shall include St Martin and the Beggar,
And the Virgin helping St Thomas to mend his shirt.

## Off Weymouth

Everything perfectly placed – the full quiet moon
Moulding in wax its mussel-shells of light
Over and over the water. Falling astern,
King George's homespun resort shows off its strings
Of bright pearl bulbs. And here, the model steamer
Chugging and chugging, the symmetry of its portholes
Beyond all question, displays a tactful quota
Of passengers on deck, each with a cheek
Angled to catch the best of cool night air.
Full as a frank confession, rounded as truth,
That moon – and that salt air, those riding waves,
The heart almost too full... *Yes, I know,*
*I know. I've seen it too. Let's go below.*

# The Escaped Names

Under the cover of light, the words we choose,
The others have long since gone: and of those that remain,
Which can tell us now their original meanings?
Each venture, it seems, is an old beginning
With equipment so shot and gone that no one would think
Of staging a raid. Or, in another translation,
*Lovely enchanting language, sugar-cane,*
*Honey of roses, whither wilt thou fly?*

No end, of course, to our vocabularies,
Evasion after evasion – but who will compile
A dictionary beyond the reach of random,
The impossible esperanto which no one speaks
But all believe in? If we were fluent in that,
Surely those ancestral words would still be waiting
In the echoing belly of the horse, in the old city,
Where now there is only moonlight and scattered stone.

Meanwhile, since there must by definition
Be always at least two ways of looking at things,
Let us, like travellers, be surprised on returning
To find the familiar strange, an otherness even
In our own homes – and be happy to find, at times,
As we look out of the window we thought was a picture,
That a leaf is part of a table; the plain sky,
Simple heaven; a stone, always a stone.

# The Dart Estuary: Whitsunday

What light could be more generous than this?
A million multiples of here and now
Tingle on the face of the water, kiss after kiss.

For hours, from high on a hill, came the crackling morse
Of guns, where tiny marksmen lobbed clay disks
Up into blue, by a vivid crescent of gorse.

Lower, a steam train passed, squirting smoke in plumes
Out through steep trees. To the west, a naval band
Wrestled with a tune that wobbled in the wind's volume.

Now, near evening, the lavish boats
Nod to the last of themselves. Along the shore,
In oil-green shadows, a hazy stillness floats.

The silence hums, a treasure-house of each
Glint of sound, where all the colours melt
To gold and then to blankness, uncoined speech.

Mast-high already, springing clear above,
The wafery moon swells to its own calm gloss,
Subsuming every language under love.

# The Artist at 81

Plain truth has become his only ornament,
Beguilement, first nature. With one white handkerchief
He will conjure the real world! Each hydra hand
Will meet the span required.

His repertoire goes down like a favourite meal:
His mind and heart savour the exact weight
Of all the notes, as one by one they ripen
Each in its own tempo.

It does not surprise him that the audience weeps:
Long ago, tears were the motherland
Of all his craft, twins to the blinding gems
Pinned to a tyrant's chest.

In this, his fine economy of age,
Nothing is show. Simply his music spells
A fluency of blessing to drown out
The worst of history. He need not even look
To know that we are weeping.

# NEW POEMS

# What do you think...?

What do you think
That your poems could ever
Open into? A clearing
As orderly as the picnic
You envisage enjoying in it?
A calm, sky-bearing lake?
A declaration of love?

You may abandon rhyme,
You may retire to receding
Points of suspension and yet...
And yet there will always be
The perfect enclosure beyond.
The dark forest. The undertow.
The heart's final stillness.


# Proofs

Delete leaves, the hum of long evenings, light.
Change to bold the grip of frost, black nights.
Rearrange forest gales, seas steep as stairs.
Italicise the stinging slopes of rain.
Stet the murderous world, heartland of despair.
Indent: in the beginning, begin again.

Insert an asterisk over Bethlehem.
Replace damaged characters with wise men.
Substitute stable for inn, manger for bed.
Transpose caviar and crust, fish and hook.
Realign hope, cherish the hungry and the dead.
Print: weigh in your hand spring's budding book.

## Voyage

They are setting out onto
The water with ease, as if
They knew or did not know
What darkness lies beneath
Their dimpled mirror-image.
Wearing their broad hats,
They nod now and smile.

Three friends, it seems, sharing
A mutual confidence – one
With hands on hips, in the prow,
Mock figurehead; one is sitting,
Hands in her lap, gazing
Serenely into the water;
One, in the sternsheets, fishes.
Her arm rests on the gunwale.

Perhaps not three, but one
So confident as to suggest
Successive poses and leave
The soft air printed with each –
One grace, one fate lifted
Across the current. In the hold,
One chance before the cold.

# Flight 000

It sags, the bright machine,
From level to level, swooping
Down beneath the canopy
Not of sky but forest.

Not clouds, but green boughs
Flick and snap at the windows,
Grazing the glass like rain
On through the avenue of trees.

And all this time, vainly,
The meticulous self-adjustments,
The throttling up and down,
The engines' whining obedience...

And this is the dream's substance –
Not the crash that must come,
Not the brute brunt in which
Limbs are a scattered luggage –

But this: the silver body
Perfect, graciously tilting
Along the narrowing flightpath.
Its illusory odyssey.

# The Bell-Buoy

Out past the cliff's redoubts
And the listing deck of the beach
Where the smart winds abduct
Our evolved words, it is hardly
The waves that stir, you'd say,
But something hidden under
That flexes, swells, slurs,
Scuds and trawls – the surface
Being only appearance
Like that thick lacqueur of sunlight
That floods the faring sea –

So with the bell-buoy, although
It remarks itself with drapes
Of weed and gaudy rust
And, in its iron ribs,
With the beat of the breathing bell
Jauntily syncopating
The undertow – yet it stands
For something else, unseen,
The sunken risks that are
Inimical to landfall:
Its only help is warning.

For lolling trippers' boats
It witnesses the point
Of turning back, at which
The heart grows calm again,
The land larger. But once
In a blue moon, in a flat
Calm, there is nothing but
A basking silence, the base
Of the buoy slowly turning –
And the questions come: what
Is absent? What is this warning?

# Recurrent

The rocking-horse stands in the hall:
You want to ride it and when you do
Your parents ride away from you.

The matron here is very tall
And creaks a little. Though she's trim
Her mouth is tight and rather grim.

The voice is shrill but when she tries
To charm you – *Just drink up your milk* –
It goes all smooth and soft like silk.

When you arrive you want to ride
The rocking-horse. You have to queue:
That of course is how they get you.

Barred gate, small trees along a drive
That dips, then rises. Your mind won't let
This image fade, or you forget.

They cure the children's nightmares – *Only
A week or two, it won't take long* –
But what child can tell the time of wrong?

The rocking-horse is never lonely –
You ride it every night and then
Your parents ride away again.

# Acts of Will

Father, son and daughter strapped
Like dummies into our rearing seats,
We are together in the plane
By an act of will entitled
*The Family's Last Holiday Before*
*The Fledglings Fly The Nest.*

And the aeroplane itself is one
Colossal dream of an iron will –
Shuddering to overcome
Every instinct of gravity,
Lifting what must fall, compressing
What must fly apart.

High up, the sun stabs from blue:
In the children's eyes, a bright joy
As they survey beneath us
Rumpled duvets of cloud.
How shall I not bring us all down
With the dull weight in my heart?

When we land, I know it is
By an act of will called simply
*Not Yet*, that my children
Do not walk away for ever,
Or dismiss the pretence of landing here
At the time that we left home.

# Rain at Sea

It rings the raddled waves, pocking
The long troughs with icy shot,
Replacing the horizon deftly
With its cold, sea-rain ghosts –

Of the captain pinned in the tall wheelhouse,
His pinched and bearded face that peers
Onto sheer disasters, the oncoming truth
Of irrefutable, house-high crests;

Of the green cabin-boy, so pale
And pretty, felled by sea fever,
Tipped from under the ensign, in the lee
Of the Horn, the crew on deck, grim-faced;

Of the ship that steers through every weather,
Doubling the Cape of Immoderate Hope,
Wheel lashed, bound for the shores of
Dark Narragonia, Never-Never...

The rain, the seething rain that falls
Knows more of soft corruption than any
Churning depth. The sea's decks,
Awash, grow wormy as any wreck.

# The Ravaged Place

*(after Klee)*

A mad skewed cone of ice,
A dunce-roof of disgrace:
It is here you told a lie
And could not show your face.

At night the air constructs
Raw blue and green around it:
You have never seen this place,
Yet long ago you found it.

The windows suck and suck
The light away. The door
Is silted up with dark:
Darkness on every floor.

It cuffs the sky, a tower
Of shrunken hurt whose name
Is that of a child gone missing
In a landscape of wobbly games.

The black wind here will blow
For ever, and each cross mark
What might have been before
The ice came down in the dark.

# Topical

This is the wilderness. We recognise it
By the surrounding park. It has no monkeys.
The locusts and the appropriate honey are gone.
Its sunlit contours murder every echo.
All sound is clamped to the head like earphones.

Under the juniper tree, the only hope
Is that of death, with no encouraging angel
To dream of. And never a drop of fatness to fall
Onto the dwellings, the dwellings marooned in the wilderness
Where no voice cries, where all the valleys stay level.

The surrounding park does not have any monkeys.
The locusts have no echo. The encouraging angel
Dreams of nothing. Neither honey nor fatness
Are appropriate. Clamped to the head, earphones echo
The exact repetitions of history. This is the wilderness.

# Early Service

Seen from behind, billowed and billowed
By his working elbows, after the blessing,
The priest's fine surplice was hardly credible –
All that washing and drying of silver,
Such energy of cotton, of elbows. And the clang
Of the paten and chalice seemed almost to ring
Untrue: as much an admission of wrong
As the view to be had at the altar rail
Of grey flannel trousers beneath the cassock
And perfectly ordinary secular shoes.

It was all secrets, a peek-a-boo glimpse
Between fingers, as the priest and server
Cruised past, crunching the dust like sugar.
And nobody knew at all what it came to,
That final huddle in the vestry after
The prayer they whispered: that conspiracy of counting.
How many coins stacked up into Babels?
How many sweets or buttons discarded?
They worked in the yellowest possible light.
Outside, dawn warded the winter darkness.

# Skull

Helmet of bone
Bronzed with lichens,
The art of the possible
Seems still to hide
In your dark sockets,
The gone nosepiece.

Superfluous, you guard
The voided citadel:
Long ago they left,
Those sly defenders
Whose best form
Was always attack.

What matters now
Is quite beyond
Your scuttled casing,
Lodged already
In other minds
Or buried in books:

Even, perhaps,
Such deathless words as
*I'll love you, always,*
Though *Faugh! Faugh!*
Is the sound of the wind
In your imperfect jaw.

# Mandelstam's Bundle

*The word is a bundle and meaning sticks out of it in
various directions*

OSIP MANDELSTAM

In the direction
Of a tramp's belongings
The kerchief economy
Of common ground
The direction of hope

In the direction
Of vulnerable nerves
To be soothed and healed
At the least touch
The direction of love

In the direction
Of a mine's triggers
To explode in the face
Of a passing tyrant
The direction of justice

In the direction
Of the word's own authority –
Lictors of logos!
Binders of beauty!
The direction of truth

In the direction
Of names to be honoured
The one double meaning
Of Mandelstam
The direction of courage

# Going Under

White, as you would think, but unkind –
A lack of grace. Nothing could prevent
The necessary needle from finding
Its mark. I remember, blurring behind,
A smile awry on a leaning face.

Chloroformed, flowers fold to sleep.
Smothering heat. Somewhere, a clatter
Much like the bang of a falling heap
Of pans. The canteen? Tinny, cheap.
Why, at that, does the heart miss a beat?

White, as you'd think – and the bed, the bed
Wheeled away now. It springs across
Joins and strips. Close to the head,
Children patting blankets. Leaden
Lids. Accepted – everything, anyhow.


# Rose Garden
*(for Matthew)*

Whorl upon whorl, cake-petals
Without charity, pale, brittle,
They flare on their barbed poles.

Brazen as searchlights, they stare
Into the angles, their field of fire
Spreads from the foot of the tower.

Stepping up to them, you sense
How they suck the air, microphones
Themselves blank, without fragrance.

Why do they flourish, where these walls
Lay down the law? Why, still tremble
At boots mashing the gravel?

Orderly, yes – and implying
Dreams of escape. Beyond them, the high
Walls lean in on the sky.

## Heroic Roses

The soft steel of moonlight never
Breaks through this forest. Only green
Plunders and narrows the dank air,
Only dark birds inch intently
Deep in its gathering rummage of growth.

But even here, so far beneath
The flickering patches of sky, at the verge
Where memory fades back to history and
The rose becomes the idea of the rose –

They are here, actual, heroic, the velvet
Of blood, their fragrance a giddying sweetness:
Whose thorns are sharp as steel, whose hearts,
Inviolate, are soft with what
They know of death and the far moon.

# Sea Song

Sometimes the seaman can understand
How the whole rocking prism of the storm
Is a function of sickness – raging light and
Ragged rearing water that pours
The dripping length of his telescope, blearing
And blurring the shape of the view with fear.

But this is not the gigantic detail
Of a real storm, with stanchions buckled,
Lights banged out and gear failing –
This is worse, this is loss of luck
Or nerve, the ship racing blindly beneath
A wrecked sky to the black reef.

Understanding cannot recaulk
The deck that is splitting under his feet,
Or bring him safe to his home port.
Sometimes, though, in dreams he reaches
A porthole moon, opens it and
Finds his anchorage, love's dry land.


# Chameleon Song

Against red – a robin, or Santa's sleeves,
A scatter of peppercorns on oiled green leaves,
Or the blood no grief retrieves;

Against yellow – starlight thick as yolk
Pouring past the hunched grey headstones, to soak
The grave no birth revokes;

Against brown – public as hope or dust,
Soft as a cow's eye, fine as hourglass rust,
Time that no heart can trust;

Against blue – the night's tall inky drapes,
The cursive blue of children's dreams, those shapes
No quick feet can escape;

Against all these, though hard to see, may move
The old chameleon, in air still crammed, above
God grounded, the hard rebirth of love.


## Purple
*(for Pauline Stainer)*


It is the precise
Blur of the fact
Being more than itself –
The smudge of corolla
Which is not detached
And does not belong.

And what are those acts
Of purple penitence
And royal mourning
But the quickening heart
Of imagination
Bearing with loss?

You wear it as if
On principle, almost –
It will always be
(Even if only
An earring) somewhere
About you, like a clue.

Like the word discovered,
Like the beating image
Held steady, that may
Yet spill over
Its own border
Into true silence.

# In the South

Why should it cause tears,
This old city with the blinds pulled down
At noon across its ochre façades,
And the birds wheeling and wheeling
Above its high towers?

It is too heavy, the knowledge
Of its fallen pediments, cracked inscriptions,
The oleanders grey with dust,
The copper pipe hollow
In the fountain's dry bowl.

All too predictable, also –
The ruins, the camera gawky on its tripod
Of yellow wood, the child wandering
Wide-eyed, ungoverned, with hand
Outstretched for money or food.

It was always there, the city,
Its first twisting thoroughfare marked
In blood from the womb. Above Troy One,
Troy Two: beyond Jerusalem,
The streets of New Jerusalem.

And who, after all, would not weep
At such an endless rebuilding? But for joy,
For the flowering city that haunts our dreams
With its sky-reflecting glass,
Its endlessly gesturing fountains.

## Concert-Going

Ours is a history
Of third parties:
Usually a full
Orchestra. At least
A soloist. Sometimes
The conspiracy
Of a wise quartet.

Whatever it is
That the music mediates,
Always it feels
Like sliding forward
And down from the chair's
Stubbed jetty
Into an ocean:

An ocean where words
Are water-gagged
And what we share
Is that privilege of
Being handed along
On the same heartbeat,
The same tugging tide.

And what we say
Must be how we listen,
And how we ride
The swell must be
As rhythmical as
The drift downwards
Of a drowning man.

And then, sometimes,
Scanning your smile,
I surmise landfall
And think to hear
Like distant cymbals
Surf exploding
On a far shore.

# Out of Land

Contained in this expansive privacy,
The hull nudged by tides, the world appears
Secure as the bleached decking, the halyards coiled
And cleated at the mast. For sure, morale
Arranges itself as simply as light and shade...
Until, on some unknowable day, there comes
A notion of land, that old affinity.

At first, a mere perversity of the water –
The swift run in, the luscious soft embrace,
A squirt into rich dark coves, a dusting of air
Where spray flings finely up from rock and blow-hole.
By logical extension, then, the trees
Arcing across the sparkling sand – the bay,
The gaudy parakeets, the trapped lagoon.

And soon the exile's fervent civics stem
All rainstorms. When the sea-fret clears the bay
It leaves, spick in bright sun, a noble polis
Whose hundred towers all speak a single language –
Whose sons, it will be said, shall never dream
Disloyalty, but whose pale eyes already
Reflect the tumbling deserts of the sea.

# Calm Sea at Night

Darkness instinct with life
Where beacons wink like cats –
Below the horizon they seem
Soft as torchlight shone
Through skin: diffuse, precious.

Love, it must be, or at least
Seduction – the trailing trills
Of phosphorescence glinting
In the water's wicked chuckles
As it collapses into whirlpools.

Tender on the face, the wind
Blows steadily, a pressure
To be trusted, a clean whistle
Of salt, entirely innocent
Of the earth's night-time coldness.

Each masthead light parades
Its triumph of pride across
The viscous, quickening sea
Where all engines turn
In a self-forgetting sleep:

And the moon, when at last it breaks
Free from the trawling clouds
Can do nothing, pale and swollen
As it is, but carry over
Our dreams to the coming dawn.

## Priest Dreams
*(for Erica)*


Again and again they kiss the priest.
He is still silly with sleep and sits
Rubbing his eyes, like a tubby child.
Behind stained glass, the lights of candles
And joyous singing, where the smiling crowd
Collects its food, the body and blood.
A grinning cook tempts me to eat
A cream cake which I cannot afford.

In other dreams, I see him hunched
Like an old chesspiece in the darkened church:
And, over his shoulder, the glowing letters
Of the book at which he mildly gazes.
The tall gladioli which shoot at his side
Have the colour of apricots speckled with blood.



## The Fish
*(for John Halkes)*


Deeper and slower the fish moves,
Each inch swum is gain of what
Already is sensed – the grain of each
Criss-crossing current, the rise and fall
Of every dot the ocean sieves
Nearer and nearer to nevermore.

Heavier, older, it cruises forward
Arrowing the tonnage of salt aside,
Letting the element work in its teeth –
Kyle of flesh, it flows between
Eternity and now, catching the light
Sometimes like sudden fire on its scales.

# Perspective

Another Annunciation – the soft entreaty
Against a triptych of windows. But who could form
An angel from that black moth wildly beating
Behind the closed door?

No artist quite contains the landscapes locked
In these embrasures – the geraniums, not lilies
Spilling from the prosperous breastpockets
Of well-cut balconies;

Or, in the middle window, the path that winds
Towards the rosy castle – where in dead ground
Children must ignore the talking birds and find
Their way past slavering hounds;

Or the third – an arrowed brightness, heading through
Sunlight lost in shafts, past chiming cattle
High above the honed spire lapped in scales, to
The point at which, looking back,

You might see a true annunciation – the world
Innocent as an egg on public view,
Nested unbroken beneath the empyrean furls
Of Mary's immaculate blue.

## On the Beach

How can you walk on the beach and not think of death,
With water welling in the corner of the dark mussel's eye
And each ribbed dish of scallop offering its portion
Of sand? And when, uphill as it seems from the beach,
The rounding swell of the sea is a still, intent brightness
Where boat after boat has its sails and its shrouds hanging slackly...

Today the clouds have reflections, their broad tarpaulins
Ride on the salt silence with a sheen of repose,
Part of a landscape from which grief and anger have ebbed
To leave nothing more than this simmering light in which thinking
Of death is not grievous, but has all the sweetness of insight.
Behind you, left and right are written in sand.


## Her Present

The dream begins again. Here is her father
Sitting glumly astride the rusting fence
While she rides round him on her motorbike,
The sunlight glittering on the sequined dress
She's wearing without reason, without rhyme,
Although she thinks she got it as a present.

The dream has trapped her in its lasting present
In which the past belongs still to her father:
Her life, she feels, will never chime or rhyme
But leave her, like her father, on the fence
And wondering whether to sell the sequined dress –
Or should she, rather, trade in the motorbike?

As usual, no answer. The motorbike,
Though little more than scrap, was once a present
As, come to that, was also the sequined dress...
Dare she escape? And should she tell her father
The time has come to climb down off the fence
And try to live as neatly as a rhyme?

There was a time, it seems, when simple rhyme
Sufficed – a time before the motorbike,
When no one sat, dejected, on the fence
And when her mother really could present
More than a pious memory to her father.
She seemed to recall the sunlight on her dress.

The dream is quite relentless, will never dress
The truth in beauty, or her thoughts in rhyme.
If only she could stop, or give her father
A token of her love – the motorbike
If necessary, or some other present.
Anything to get him off the fence...

It always happens like this: suddenly, the fence
Gone, the stormwind tearing at her dress,
The vortex that sucks down the past, the present,
The future – all that time can ever rhyme.
No possible escape! The motorbike
Vanishes into dust, bearing her father.

There is no fence, the air can never rhyme
With sequins or her dress. The motorbike
Is no more present than is her absent father.

# By the Canal
*(for Catriona)*


She had done nothing wrong, but her guilt
Gleamed blackly on the slack surface

She had done nothing wrong, but her shame
Stood in judgement from the high poplars

She had done nothing wrong, but her tears
Stung her cheeks raw in the smoking sunlight

She had done nothing wrong, but her breath
Blurted and blurted in the drenching dew

She had done nothing wrong, but her mind
Could not escape from the jumbled hulk

Of the sunlight, the trees, the water,
The terrible guilt at the nothing she had done.


# Wreath


Down from the steep grey decks it falls,
A gaudy lifebelt banging flat onto
Small waves, the fragrant fifth
Of a sonnet, *O bleu* that the blue ocean haunts.

Dying, already the leaves are curling,
Pitted with acid: the sweet-smelling cram
Of lilies and roses sucks at salt
And rust blooms at the wire's bright core.

Until, miles from land, the bees
Home to sip this sweetness which
For a moment stems the long tides –
Honey salvaged from the darkest sea.

# Driving Westward

*(for my mother)*

For Polesworth now read Holsworthy: on Radio Three,
Continuity, Dowland's sighing tears. Each tree
Wields its true flail, the Atlantic wind's corrective:
The rusts that gnaw the hedgerow look infective.
By Germansweek and Ashwater, low mist,
A scrim of green, the threadbare rain persisting,
The fields unleavened by light. Here and there,
A horse and rider draggling in the drenched air.
So it is that, driving towards the west,
I think of the poet's impulse towards the east
Which now the mirror shows as a grey and thin
Oblong where car-lights grow larger or diminish –
The occasional driver grimly making way
White-faced and frowning into the blinding spray.
To imagine the poet imagining God I find
A fine enough conceit, even a kind
Of consolation – as if, simply by driving
In the same direction on the same day could imply
An echo of faith, a journey back and on
Under a sky on fire with that long gone
Certainty. Now as then a poet must
Make the best of what is to hand and trust
To his luck lasting – and even en route to friends,
Remember to honour means as much as ends.
As if...I stare at the screen, its constantly blurring
Transparent Jackson Pollocks wiped off, recurring
(Frank O'Hara declared the artist to be
'Tortured with self-doubt, tormented by anxiety')
And try to focus on what there is to glean
From what there is, the collapsed cartography
Of faith's projections. And now my memory
Races ahead to where that western sea
Floods, ebbs and is steady beyond those hills
And valleys bright with kingcups, daffodils,
The blackthorn's small white stars – and there, one small
Boat is fishing, its blue hull rising, falling

Across the muscular swell...As if the weight
Of hills and oceans might be mediated
By one small flower, the merest bobbing ounce
Of fishhook fortune. Meanwhile, John Donne dismounts,
Keeping God at his back, content to know
The journey done, the poem safely stowed.

## Old Man Dying
*(in memory of Patrick Campbell)*


The whole bay, like a rich skin
Puckers at his touch, dips like silk
As huge, at home, he wades in.

I know it cannot be quite true –
He is not here, but on the hill,
Counting for safety to see him through

Dying – but here, his premature ghost
Baptises itself, mastering death
On a gentle Lilliputian coast.

An old man who dips and wades
Past the hour of his mortal strength,
Back bent now, the body splayed...

And at the side of the cot, his hand
Lifts. The water folds across.
Unseen, perhaps he steps onto dry land.



## Anchor


Hope plucked
From the misty mud,
All its paid out
Scope is hauled
To the bitter end.

A blessing, an icon,
It rises to light
Through bubbled pressures
And the fish flat
As pressed flowers.

Firstling of
The imagination,
Already it drifts
Free beneath
The boat going on.

Great grey hook,
Even when landed
On deck it keeps
The look of clear,
Ancient depths.

Lastage of
The imagination,
Chained to the live
Hull of history
It holds fast.

## Paysages Moralisés

1

St George's eve – the elderly relatives brave
A cold April breeze, the twin uncertainties
Of pain and a world increasingly unbecoming.
But circling the Town Hall, by some swift magic we wave
Goodbye and cross a sunlit threshold into
The working model of a full-scale English spring.

Everything is impossibly in place –
The bluebell woods, their broad mauve-blue smudges
Never quite in focus, always bestowing
Too late, as we pass, a corporate vision of grace.
A mile on, the opening over of the village season,
The bowler lumbering up, unfit and blowing.

There is even a bride by the Thames, frilly and stiff,
Marooned for photos on a little island of grass,
Standing between two bridesmaids with bouquets.
Later, a hotel tea – and then we drift
Homewards, the car purring easily beneath
Aisles of blossom rocketing in high sprays.

Lost in the hollow acoustic of a dream, my mother
And aunt are borne along – beguiled, but no longer
Convinced by ancient emblems such as these.
Seeing, for one thing, the bowler's clenched fist: for another,
That bridal dress brittle as icing, as ready to snap
As the mantrap half hidden by the bluebells' tender leaves.

2

Grand high billows, Constable cloud
And, far beneath, an eyepiece made
From perfect hedgerows, arching trees.
Summer is a natural art, its peepshows
Aimed at infinity's parallel poles.

We look down on a hayfield pale
And razored as any in the quilted counties
Of southern England. Under the haze,
An atmospheric that the working gears
Of distant machines can hardly parse.

The car creaks as it cools. Lunch
Is exemplary, laid out inch by inch –
Fluted spring onions, carmine radishes,
Ham, lettuce, tomatoes, bread
And wine. The rug hugs the slope of the field.

The picnicker's art is deftly to fold
Past and future into the shape
Of now: in genuine hampers, to ship
The freight of leisure to the open air,
To remake Elysium from things as they are.

But try as we may, something has faltered.
No version of pastoral can filter
Justice from beauty: its silver tongue
Cannot hope to delay for long
The storm looming, the weight that has massed

Outside the frame and surely must
Burst any moment. We pack and drive straight
Back to the city. Beggars. The streets
Padlocked. Cardboard shelters. Time
Beating like a held bird, longing to fly.


# Medlar
*(for Antoinette & John Moat)*


Its ball of fossil wool
Looks brittle as butterscotch.
Growing its own graphs,
It knits and knots, crazily
Involuted, high voltage,
Crackling with complications,
A fist held up, stripped down
To all its wires of muscle.

Still, in front of your house,
Its outline can sometimes be
A simple circle on a stem
As if time could relent
Or a family tree finally
Round to O, to home.

## On Remembrance Day
*(for Charlie)*


The golden rages of autumn,
Each immolated tree doused with sun
And set on fire

But not there, at the heart
Of the wood, in the weighty quiet acoustic
Of its lumbered room

There, death can be followed
Precisely, its every step is tagged,
A shivering hawk-bell

The bell, then solid silence
Ringing in the ear. The drums of pheasant-feed
Leak one grain more

The bell, softly clacking,
And already waiting at the next silence,
Squeals of pain

Later, dark wings shrug
Upwards to settle calmly on the crown
Of a tree still in flames

## Elements

It becomes in itself
A possessed medium –
The dripping musk-air
Of summer darkness,
The nervous window-frames
Clearing their throats –
Or withdraws to gesture,
Optative, flicking
A feather's hairs, then
Silent, an atmosphere
Passing through us
As it exercises,
As it bottles our words
In its wide bubble.

*

The footfall, for all
Its echo, must meet
The acoustic, dead
As adobe, which nothing
Can mitigate – pitiful
The bowls and bones
In the earth's hollows,
The earth which bears
All evidence of horror,
But that also gleams
With the springing wheat,
That barricades the sky's
Blank blue with green,
With the hopes of mortal love.

*

Paradox of flames –
Image of the flighty
Bird of hope,
But remorseless, the agent
Of mad moralities,
Requiring an exact
Rendering down
To the grey economy
Of ash: and too often
Infernal, that flickering
Brightness reflected
In our own eyes –
The books burning,
The phoenix itself consumed.


*


The world's shifting cargo,
Already it has crossed
The threshold to lap
At our little bones
With its wild choices –
To give or take
To buoy up or drown
To show or conceal
To bring home a cradle
Or the dark gliding boat –
It lies on our souls
Like an imprint of love,
Each moonstruck drop
Embracing the horizon.

# Homage to Paul Klee
*(for Pam)*


1. *Alphabet Country*

And now you are entering
Alphabet country
You may look to lodge by the red road
In Villa R. The rates are reasonable,
The food adequate, instruction free.

In general, do not
Ask too many questions.
Y, by the way, is a gulf or bird,
Also the shapes of trees in a park
Near L (Lucerne is one suggestion).

You'll soon learn the logic
Of literal vision –
C, of course, for a ship in harbour,
H for father, thus I for mother,
While B gives birth to a composition.

Some meanings, though,
Can never be amended –
W is always woe, branded
On the child's brow: Mister Z,
Grim bossman, is hardly a friend.

Above all, beware
When letters attempt
To get together. Such combinations
Are IRR (quite mad) or RIP,
Perverse analysis (is that all it meant?)

The best you can hope for
Is a four-letter code.
Example: when L is not Lucerne
It could be Lily at the piano, playing
Bach in love's authentic mode.

Other examples:
Paul, or still better
Klee – a four-leafed German clover,
A French key and an English reminder
Of N on a headstone, the final dead letter.


2. *Tunisia 1914*

Over the harbour, the ascendant heat
Bleaches all colour. Tremulous palms
Cannot protect the wide sea
Or its last hope of blue. The curvature
Of the far horizon demands acceptance.
History looms like an old repeat.

Here in the blank and burning air
Daily the sun must realise
Its fierce liquidity. Even where
The mosque can scarcely maintain its streaming
Pillar of light, each glittering grain
Of dust is part of a call to prayer.

At dusk, slowly, the landmass cools
To colour. That angles sharpen to north
And south is as natural to you
As using the left hand for drawing, the right
For writing. Beyond the black minaret
A pale green moon makes beauty still seem true.


3. *Woodlouse*

When the sea goes down into its dark low cellar
And the restaurant on the Jungfrau freezes over,
There are still fish and birds to bear their witness
To silence and speech, to the deeply sunken sky
And the ocean overhead; to the innocence of colour.

The last year of your life. Again, here comes
The absurd and dangerous drummer who cannot bend
His knees. You feel your own membranes drying out,
Tensing you towards death. The desert cacti
Slide out from silos of shade to face the heat.

You find yourself in border country again.
The woodlouse, whose armature insists on blackness,
Is a skeleton fish, is the spine of a bird's feather.
Rolled up, it mimics a charred and hollow sun,
A black lifebelt in one corner of the sea.

It is a fossil of the will, of our little dipping
Into the elements for as long as humanly possible.
The way you have painted it, it might well be a last
Holy imprint, a springboard from which to leap
Clear to a world of silent birds, fish singing.


4. *Deep in the Forest*

Beyond the shade, beyond thought,
Beyond the very thought of shade,
The green heart of the forest hums,
An intensity immune to time –
Not to be weighed or measured, though
It is the power-house, the source.

*The womb, the house, the garden gate,*
*The flower-lined path, all led you straight*
*Across the meadow into the wood*
*In whose dark ranks dark silence stood.*

Here all invitations to meaning
Are elegiac in their outline,
Although provisionally you may call
This whirling mill a dim propeller,
This microphone a sunflower head,
This falling bird a wind-loose leaf.

*You stood, then heard a distant stream*
*And ran to find it, ran till it seemed*
*Your heart would burst: then stopped. All round,*
*The sweet thick darkness, but not a sound.*

How it swells and shifts and grows,
That green intensity of dreaming,
That sighing sea at the forest's heart –
And the little adult words drift down
And down, to break open and lie
Like pale casings on the hot floor.

*Not a sound until there came*
*Those frightened voices calling your name.*
*You shivered with pleasure as you went on*
*Into the dark where you had never gone.*


## Broken Glass


Oh, it could cut us to the quick
To try to grasp those shivered shards of truth
Which never tell but show – as if each brittle
Broken fragment, if only well retrieved,
Could hold the entire landscape filmed upon it.

But nothing is more fully broken
Or so impossible ever again to believe in –
How those bits rattle in the dustpan as you sweep!
How they must be lumpily disposed
In parcels of newsprint thick enough to blunt them!

And now, gingerly reaching
Through a jagged frame of air, you find unnatural
This closeness of the fields, these ticking flowers
Across the sill; as if through a broken seal
A definition of something had leaked away.

# Departures

Set in a floral arcade,
These are the dreams of departures, in which
The ancient climbing roses are always
In bloom beneath the shivering glass
Of the station's forcing-house. Although
Figures must dwindle and twined fingers
Have to unclasp, the backward look
Stays for ever. On cheeks high-toned
With grief, a single frozen tear.

But dreams are dreams – already
The first bend has removed the station
From view, and the shapely words of thanks
And farewell no longer make sense as the engine
Rattles through landscapes to which they belong
Not at all. Accept, nonetheless,
This real ghost train of gratitude, of words
Marshalled before, to be printed after,
As the lights of the carriages shrink into darkness.

# Truth and Lies

It sometimes seems I only need to lie
Still for a moment – and in it floods, the sea
Of surging water, blue and bright as ice,
From which there is no refuge, not one rock
Or cave in which to shelter or to hide...
Yet all this happens only in my mind.

My doctor says there's nothing in my mind
Which needs attention – but that's just a lie
For all I know, a vain attempt to hide
The truth, to stem the savage rushing sea.
Sometimes I wake at night and cannot rock
Myself back to sleep: often I'm cold as ice.

The future glitters sharp as sun on ice,
It dances in the chambers of my mind –
Although the music sounds a bit like rock,
So that I prefer to sit or lie
As if I were a bather by the sea
Or spotting birds from the warm dark of a hide.

But then it is impossible to hide
The truth, although it often cuts like ice –
At some point the bather has to brave the sea,
At some point out of sight is out of mind –
But even this is better than the lie
Of the land which sags seawards in crumbling rock.

The sand upon the beach was once a rock,
I sometimes think – the doctor cannot hide
The truth or ever, go on prescribing a lie.
'My dear,' he says, 'Your fingers are like ice.
Have you considered mittens? Would you mind
Taking a winter holiday by the sea?'

Why is it that all roads lead back to the sea?
I feel the known world begin to rock,
The water table rises in my mind.
I want to flee inland, I want to hide –
If only tides could be locked up in ice –
But how can truth be thawed out from a lie?

The doctor says no sea can ever hide
The tallest rock: his words grip me like ice.
Deep in my mind, I ache for a comforting lie.

# Last Rites

For two weeks now the old man has been trying
To peel the skin from his thumb, as if it were
A stall: but cannot. He works away at it for hours.

Meal-times bring other puzzles. His own hand
Mimics the hand that feeds him, tipping spoonfuls
Of thin-air soup into air, beside his mouth.

Nights are no better. Once, they found him stark
Naked and swearing loudly among the women
And had to hold him, drug him back to torpor.

Sometimes he calls for someone – a Mr Hogg,
Though no one knows him. Sometimes, he enquires
Whether his cases have been conveyed to the palace.

His visitors sit miserably, hoping
Time will go quickly – for him, for them. The lino
Gleams and gleams, harbouring no speck of dust.


# Harbour

We have died and died into this new life,
Made peace with all the houses which we left
And long since said farewell to the *avant-garde*
Of new horizons, as to the *arrière-pensées*
Of numberless prodigal dreams...And now there is
The light leaping from water to flick across
The paintwork of houses and hulls, the unspoilt warmth
Of immediate sunlight baptising us into age.

The smell of fresh bread carries over the water.
Churchbells, laughter from pubs, the mail – small treats.
And even if nothing has quite the depth that once
We expected, here all the tides rock back to balance.
Over the cocktails, almost we could envisage
Accepting this, our fondest image of death.

## White Lilac

Even in the city's
Not quite darkness
It dazzles, this froth
Of turrets which swoop
Softly in the night's breezes.

At the edge of distance
A train scrapes by,
Its hollow aspirate
Rises and lasts,
Lasts and finally fades.

Is there nothing to this
But time passing,
The moon filling,
The flowers which exhale
Their sweet, drugging airs?

As birthday greeting
I send you this
Standstill whiteness
Of a May night, whose lingering
Fragrance goes straight to the heart.

## At the Forest Edge

Between the low slate wall
And the green pagodas
The wood's breath passes,
Its palpable cool
A musk of sap,
A dark puff of knowledge.

Its lips might take you in
Beyond sunlight:
Beyond the first few
Visible yards
You would look back
To a pale strip of brightness.

Almost before you know,
On into darkness
Is the only possible
Path to take,
Away from a world
Scribbled across, erased.

Soon you will have forgotten
Even the gorse
That drifted over
The open heath,
Its exotic whiff
Of coconut and summer.


## When

When in the far deep fathoms
The mackerel lie torpid; when
The hedgehog has curled up and dropped
Its heartbeat like a practised yogi

When the balancing seals still float
Up to their black air-holes; when
The palolo worm has long since spawned
Precisely at daybreak, in Samoa and Fiji

When the poorwill nightjar has gone
To find a rock to sleep in; when
The leaves themselves have counted down
The shortening, shortest hours of daylight

When every triangle is a tree
Or half a treetop starburst; when
All threesomes are shepherds, magi
Or mother, father and holy child

When to hibernate in a church
Might be to dream of hope; even when
Outside is only the moon's acid brightness
And cries that carry all through the night


## En Route


At dusk, above the flat lanes,
White-flecked, of the motorway, I saw
A plane that drifted up against
Great swags of purple cloud,
Its single lance of light held out
To brave the impenetrable wall
Of bruising weather. Against the towering
Bank of darkness it rose and rose.

I saw then the insect that climbs
To scour the walls of a blank room
In search of any possible exit –
Admirable, persistent, a tiny
But complete model of imagination,
Of all the possibilities of flight.

## Wedding Song
*(for Sophia and Robin)*

Perhaps even here, among the airiest moments
Of wishing, there can be pre-emptive stillness –
As when the bride, gingerly easing out
Of the limousine, pauses, with barely a foot on the ground.

Or when the double-handed knife is poised
Above the hard and soft of the cake. When the pen
Inclines to its shadow, but the nap remains unscathed.
When the bell's clapper is still sounding the air.

Or when the vocative rings are still empty,
Held at the trembling tips of fingers that soon
Will almost eclipse them. When for a moment the light
Seems to thicken to a slanting smoke of dust.

And this, perhaps, is how love stows its gifts
Away, in little trices of silence. As when
The wind just curls away to nothing and even
The everyday waves of the lake are cured of time.

# Index of titles and first lines

(Titles are in italics, first lines in roman type.)

**Lawrence Sail** was born in London in 1942 and brought up in the west country: he now lives in Exeter with his son and his daughter. He read modern languages at St John's College, Oxford, then taught in Kenya for nearly five years. After teaching in various schools, most recently Exeter School, he is now a freelance writer.

He has published five books of poems: *Opposite Views* (Dent, 1974), *The Drowned River* (Mandeville Press, 1978), *The Kingdom of Atlas* (Secker & Warburg, 1980), *Devotions* (Secker & Warburg, 1987) and *Aquamarine* (Gruffyground Press, 1988). *Out of Land: New & Selected Poems* (1992) is his first publication with Bloodaxe Books. His poems have been broadcast on radio and television, and he has presented *Poetry Now* (BBC Radio 3) and *Time for Verse* (BBC Radio 4). A former editor of *South West Review* (from 1981 to 1985), he has also compiled and edited several anthologies, including *First and Always* (Faber, 1988). He reviews for *PN Review*, *Poetry Review* and *Stand*.

He is chairman of the Arvon Foundation. In 1991 he was director of the Cheltenham Festival of Literature and in the same year one of the judges for the Whitbread Book of the Year. He was awarded a Hawthornden Fellowship in 1992.